Soul
Purpose
Astrology

W9-BPM-283

What Is Spiritual Astrology?

Spiritual astrology uses personal insight gleaned from the birth chart for spiritual development and transformation. *Soul Purpose Astrology* gives you the basic information needed to understand your life's highest purpose through your birth chart.

You will learn to read a birth chart for clues to your individual strengths, talents, and abilities, and to specific life areas in which valuable opportunities for learning may arise. Through the Nodes of the Moon, you can discover your soul's purpose in this lifetime. With this easy-to-follow introductory guide, you can also learn how to:

• Focus on your essential virtues and positive potential

• Transform negative attitudes and fear

• Develop tolerance and understanding of others' differences

• Discover your best source of empathetic intuition—heart, mind, or solar plexus

• Find out which careers or life path choices make the best use of your unique talents, interests, and skills

About the Author

Margaret Koolman (Hawaii) has studied astrology since 1975. This book grew from her teaching notes at the request of her students, who found that her style and content were not available in other books. Ms. Koolman presents workshops and readings in England, Australia, and the United States. She is available for personal readings and can be contacted through her website. Margaret's next book, *The Sacred Heart of Astrology*, written in collaboration with author Kay Snow-Davis, is almost complete.

To Write to the Author

If you wish to contact the author or would like more information about this book, please write to the author in care of Llewellyn Worldwide and we will forward your request. Both the author and publisher appreciate hearing from you and learning of your enjoyment of this book and how it has helped you. Llewellyn Worldwide cannot guarantee that every letter written to the author can be answered, but all will be forwarded. Please write to:

Margaret Koolman
℅ Llewellyn Worldwide
P.O. Box 64383, Dept. 0-7387-0221-8
St. Paul, MN 55164-0383, U.S.A.

Please enclose a self-addressed stamped envelope for reply,
or $1.00 to cover costs. If outside U.S.A., enclose
international postal reply coupon.

Many of Llewellyn's authors have websites with additional information and resources. For more information, please visit our website at http://www.llewellyn.com.

Margaret Koolman

Soul
Purpose
Astrology

How to Read
Your Birth Chart for
Growth & Transformation

2002
Llewellyn Publications
St. Paul, Minnesota 55164-0383, U.S.A.

Soul Purpose Astrology: How to Read Your Birth Chart for Growth & Transformation
© 2002 by Margaret Koolman. All rights reserved. No part of this book may be used or reproduced in any manner whatsoever, including Internet usage, without written permission from Llewellyn Publications except in the case of brief quotations embodied in critical articles and reviews.

SECOND EDITION
First Printing, 1998

(First edition published by Davies & Ritchie, 1998)

Cover design by Lisa Novak
Cover art and interior illustrations on pages 35, 37, 39, 41, 44, 46 ,49, 51, 54, 56, 59, 61
    © 2001 by Jane Mjolsness
Interior illustrations by Gavin Dayton Duffy, Llewellyn art department

Library of Congress Cataloging-in-Publication Data

Koolman, Margaret.
    Soul purpose astrology : how to read your birth chart for growth & transformation
/ Margaret Koolman.—2nd ed.
        p.   cm.
    Includes index.
    ISBN 0-7387-0221-8
        1. Predictive astrology. I. Title.

    BF1720.5 .K65 2002
    133.5—dc21   2001050830

Llewellyn Worldwide does not participate in, endorse, or have any authority or responsibility concerning private business transactions between our authors and the public.
    All mail addressed to the author is forwarded but the publisher cannot, unless specifically instructed by the author, give out an address or phone number.
    Any Internet references contained in this work are current at publication time, but the publisher cannot guarantee that a specific location will continue to be maintained. Please refer to the publisher's website for links to authors' websites and other sources.

Llewellyn Publications
A Division of Llewellyn Worldwide, Ltd.
P.O. Box 64383, Dept. 0-7387-0221-8
St. Paul, MN 55164-0383, U.S.A.
www.llewellyn.com

Printed in the United States of America

*This book is dedicated
to the unfolding of personal consciousness
toward and within that greater awareness
of the oneness of life.*

Others Books by Margaret Koolman

Soul Purpose Astrology

(First edition published by Davies & Ritchie, 1998)

Acknowledgments

Writing this book has been a process beginning twenty-seven years ago when I began to discover how wonderful life experience could be, when viewed in the light of astrological understanding. Thanks for my first reading go to Bernard Honey, who later shared the basic principles of astrology with me against the backdrop of the mystery school teaching, which encouraged depth and breadth of interpretation. In Kauai, in 1996, I was generously offered the practical support I needed to get my teaching notes into shape. My thanks go to Tom and Linda Carpenter, who teach the Course in Miracles material, and to many other people at that time, for their emotional and spiritual support. Back in England, the manuscript improved immeasurably through the kind and incisive suggestions and corrections of my dear friend Maureen Ritchie, who worked with me to completion of the book's original printed form; and my thanks go also to Graham Davies for his steady support over the years. Thank you, too, to David Cousins, whose swinging lantern lights my path ahead. I gratefully acknowledge my sons, Howard and Adrian Koolman, for their computer expertise in creating the astrology software and symbols and for their patient teaching and encouragement, and my loving thanks for their unfailing friendship that is a major joy in my life. During the last few years, I have enjoyed exploring, with author Kay Snow-Davis, the vision of astrology as the readable expression of the inexorable and beautiful evolution of human life. At this present time, I thank Llewellyn Publications for backing my original work and polishing it for more public consumption. My thanks go also to my friends and supporters all over the world, and to my clients and students who have given me "grist for the mill" through the years of my career; now I feel the inner stirrings of so much more that I wish to share with you all. The deepest gratitude that expands my heart is for life itself, the love, the joy, and the peace that is our common true being.

Foreword

Before meeting Margaret Koolman, my feelings about astrology were based upon the way many people use it as an authority outside of themselves in which to make choices in their lives. I saw too many come to believe the position of the planets was the source of either all their problems or all their opportunities, and deny the power we all have within ourselves to choose the direction of our life. Astrology, however, is merely a tool, and the value of this tool depends entirely upon the astrologer's purpose and skill.

I know and love Margaret for the depth of her spiritual awareness, which is extraordinary, and I see that the way she shares her high level of consciousness is through astrology, helping others find their own greater awareness as well. Knowing that an astrological chart is not the cause of anything, but a mirror of our own past choices and present options, Margaret helps us realize how the pieces of our experience can lead to the unity of our whole spiritual Being. Through her interpretations of astrology, she empowers us as spiritual Beings having a physical experience, leading us to an expanded awareness of the purpose of the choices and opportunities we have.

To me, Margaret would be a wonderful teacher of higher consciousness in any form she chose. *Soul Purpose Astrology* is a beautiful expression of both her awareness, and her astrological skills.

—Linda Carpenter
Teacher of *A Course in Miracles*
Publisher of *Dialogues of Awakening*

Contents

Preface

I discovered that my grandmother had been an astrologer when I received some of her books from my father after she had died. At the time I was studying the great philosophers of the past and discovering the dubious pleasure of finding flaws in other people's thinking. I was a cynic and was determined to find the flaws in astrology as well. I knew that to bring any system down, one needs to study it first, and the weaknesses reveal themselves to the discerning mind. So I studied astrology at a basic level and began to practice the principles through the charts of my friends.

I discovered that I could find out things about them that they had never revealed to me before, and I realized that, whatever flaws there may be, astrology actually works. For me, at that point, "the Earth shook," and I stopped bothering to try to disprove philosophies and began the great and joyful exploration of understanding myself and other people.

A birth chart reading can be a wonderful and enlightening experience. At best, the recipients of such a reading gain a sense of complete acceptance, of doors opening to endless possibilities, of previous emotional pain becoming positive, hopeful experience, and of relief, both of finding themselves and also of feeling recognized by the universe.

When a reading is insensitively given, it can be a shock and can leave the recipients doubtful of their value and apprehensive about the future. Such impressions can be alleviated and dispersed by a vision of our place within the whole, and the realization that every lesson in life can be negative or positive, depending entirely on whether our attitude to life is of "a glass half empty" or "a glass half full"; closed and protective, or open and growing.

The introduction of this book begins with my philosophical approach to the whole of life, which is not, in itself, a part of astrological principles, but rather underlies the way I apply those principles to the questions of How? and Why? about our life as part of existence as a whole. It is not essential to read the introduction first. A beginner in astrology might prefer to start with "Astrology in a Nutshell" in chapter 1 or "The Zodiac Story" in chapter 2.

Throughout the book, the principles of Zodiac signs, planets, and houses will be presented many times in different ways. Looking from different perspectives, a fuller picture gradually emerges, replacing a beginner's confusion with greater and greater clarity. The basic astrological principles are explored, and the method of using them for positive benefit is demonstrated with many examples.

There are exercises given at many points, encouraging the reader to think about experience from different directions. Many of these exercises consist of questions, and as every person is different, there will be many different ways of answering them. All answers that you come up with are valid for you. The questions are designed as a process that will draw out both your inner knowledge of what is right for you, and your intuitions for others.

Even a little understanding, wisely used, can be valuable. Like a small torch in the dark, it may not show the entire scene at a glance, but it can save you from tripping over your less useful habits, and possibly even help you see where you are going.

Introduction

The most significant personal moment, in terms of our life as spirit on Earth, is the moment of birth, the birth of our own separate, individually tailored set of equipment, our earthly body. As spirit, we had been hovering around the body of the mother, gathering this fetus as a set of faculties, or tools, for perceiving and interpreting our experience, and at some point committing ourselves to the coming life.

At the moment of birth, this little body is cut loose from the womb, that reminder of universal Oneness. The threshold is crossed and our earthly experience begins: the quality of that beginning is reflected in everything around us.

Beginnings set the scene for what follows, so if we map the heavens at the birth moment of any person, group, or project, we can learn something of the context and qualities to be unfolded. These maps are two-dimensional charts of the three-dimensional universe, and "astrology" is the interpretation, according to specific principles, of charts drawn for significant moments of time.

Everything in the world around us reflects us, and the world is moving, changing, and reacting, as we are ourselves. The only movement that is regular and predictable is that of the "celestial lights." So, looking at the chart of a chosen moment can give reliable feedback, and the system of meaning used has been established over many hundreds of years. Generally, the celestial lights astrologers choose to chart are the Sun, Moon, and planets; sometimes distant stars and galaxies are included as well as certain asteroids. The belt of sky that contains the Sun, Moon, and planets is divided into twelve Zodiac signs to define planetary positions.

To the person viewing the heavens, its appearance at any moment can express that moment entirely; it shows us a pattern, or matrix, that relates to every aspect of that moment in every dimension in which experience is possible, from our spiritual source to the appearance of the physical world around us. The pattern of our birth chart represents the matrix of our life as a separate being, and can be interpreted at any level.

So, every dimension of a person's experience can be found in their birth chart, and the particular interpretation given depends on the level of focus of the interpreter.

For the physical level of a reading, an astrologer refers to the planets as indicators of events, people in our lives, and the state of our physical body. The twelve divisions of the circle from the vantage point of the Earth, called *houses*, represent areas of daily life. For instance, career is seen in the tenth house, which is the highest part of the sky at the top of the chart. Earnings are seen in the second house, partnerships in the seventh house, and so on.

On the level of vital energy, the pattern of planetary energies shows our health through the organization of our energy system, and shows what experience we attract through the energy we give out.

On the emotional level, we read, through the chart, about emotional reactions and tendencies. Who or what sparks them off can be suggested by using the houses.

On the mental level, we are dealing more with attitudes, which are assumed and often unconscious, or learned, cultivated characteristics.

On the soul level, we are looking at the highest potential of the characteristics shown by the planetary arrangement, and our chosen purpose for this particular life. Spiritually, we can regard each planet as representing an archetypal energy principle of human life, and the Zodiac itself as twelve faces of God in human form shining through the human heart. For each life, our spirit chooses one Sun sign as the quality of human heart through which to radiate.

Almost the whole of our conscious experience is of Time unfolding. There can be moments, between heartbeats, when we recognize the eternal infinity of timelessness, but normally we each relate to our world through the varied vibrations of our own personal senses. Each conscious experience we have elicits a response, an internal action, and this is likely to become an unconscious reaction in later circumstances that appear to us the same. What has happened before, we expect to happen again, and we prepare ourselves for it.

We each read the world in our own way, actually perceiving what we have come to expect and reacting to it again. Within Time, we experience many lifetimes as individual forms, and every lifetime adds to our accumulation of expectations. The result is that we interpret most of what we see in terms of these conditioned expectations, and so the surroundings that we perceive reflect that conditioning back to us. The spirit that we are has very little chance of interfering in all this; sometimes, even when we suspect that things may be different from what they seem to be, we have great difficulty not reacting in the same old way.

However, when we are in touch with our spiritual self, we can see clearly, because in truth it is all spirit anyway; our spiritual light reflected in the world shows us a vision of completeness, deep value, and true meaning, where the reality of Oneness shines through diversity, on one level dissolving it. One way to be in touch with these clear reflections of spirit is to become familiar with those reactions and responses of ours that obscure them. As we become aware of the extent to which our life experience is due to our personality perspective, we realize that we ourselves are clouding what we are looking at. When we look again with that in mind, the way is open for that clear vision, and we can consciously recognize that all things are truly spirit.

Ways of Looking at Birth Charts

It is very important to be aware that we are not formed or affected by our birth chart any more than land is formed or affected by a map we may draw of its features. Our birth chart can be interpreted as a map of the world the way we personally tend to understand it. In giving us a picture of our personal way of perceiving our life, the chart confirms our experience. We may also realize that things may be different for others, which will be seen from their birth charts. This confirmation of our personal experience helps us know and accept our personality as it is, and it is our greater, or higher, self that is doing the accepting—the personality is not all we are.

Just by looking at our birth chart, we take the position of observer. The emotional clinging to experience drops away for a moment, revealing a clearer vision of ourselves as spirit clothed in personality. In relationships, once we realize the extent of our assumptions about other people, we can start to wonder who they really are and relate to them directly.

One way we can use our birth chart is to help us locate our negative attitudes and feelings. As we begin to understand them, the aspect of our character that has defended itself with them reveals to us its essential virtues, and they can then be integrated. Another way we can use the chart is to focus on our positive potential so that we grow more consciously into all that we can be, rather than giving energy to our habitual smallness. A third way to use the birth chart, on receiving the astrological confirmation of our personality structure, is to identify ourselves with the higher self and let the spirit shine through that personality, which naturally brings out its best.

Astrology can help us develop tolerance and understanding of people by showing us how very different our personalities are. Our birth charts give clues as to what the differences are and how the consequent experiences feel; they are like mirrors of our individual personalities. As you would look in the glass to see if your hair is as you wish it, or check that there is no cabbage leaf in your teeth from lunch, so you can look into your astrological birth chart to check whether you are "being yourself" or are caught in some role leftover from past pressures, like the need to survive, to be successful, or to conform.

Through your chart, you can check the accuracy of your empathic intuition, finding whether it works better for you to trust responses from your mind, your heart, or your solar plexus; and you can find out in which circumstances you are liable to make mistakes.

You can also determine your best career, given your particular talents and skills, and discover whether that career will really give you all the satisfaction you want, or whether you also need a more personal form of service.

You can see how you choose behavior in accordance with your expectations of other people's motives and opinions, and how that creates the experience you have with those people and with the world at large. If your relationships tend to have similar outcomes, you can discover why.

Children—The Process of Birth

When you look into the mirror of a child's personality, you will know better what kind of encouragement to give. Although similar in many ways, children have very different personalities from each other from the first moments of life. There are so many combinations possible of all the information that makes up a birth chart that the only time two people will have the same combination is when they are born at the same time in the same place. Even with twins born within moments of each other, those few minutes make a difference. Comparisons of people who were born at similar times but were not brought up together, show many identical timings of events, coincidences of names, and other odd similarities, but basically they are still different people.

Children possess their basic character potential from before birth and a predisposition to react to their parents a certain way, all of which can be seen in their birth chart. Yet they also have their inheritance of genes and DNA, and the upbringing that will occur due to the parents' life circumstances and experience (like the degree of financial wealth and the nationality), and these things cannot be seen astrologically.

Between lives, although we still continue to identify individually, we withdraw from the vision of material separation, so it is easier to see that separation is ultimately not real. Many spirits are drawn to create physicality again through the desire for some experience they remember; and some come into the physical dimension with the purpose of maintaining the spiritual perspective and the desire to help other people do the same. Perhaps we are pulled into, or choose, earthly life at a particular time for our spirit to fulfill the needs of that time and of those parents. There are as many purposes to incarnate as there are people, and, although a birth chart reveals an enormous amount about a person, it cannot show the individual spirit.

As spirit creating a life of earthly experience, we choose those abilities that will help us fulfill this life's purpose. We have a vast fund of experiences from the past through which we have developed those abilities, but, in the lives where they were developed, we will have had difficulties that were not solved and relationships that needed balancing, together with attitudes and habits that are not necessarily relevant to this life, and all that must come with the chosen abilities. So our particular blend of characteristics may not be what we would consciously choose from our present, relatively limited viewpoint.

As our spirit extends itself, the physical, emotional, and mental conditions of our particular parents and upbringing are attracted through the vibration of our purpose and the character it requires; the incoming vibration creates the earthly circumstances that receive it. The new baby, when responding to each experience, draws on the qualities and programming that its spirit has brought, and this pulls the personality into incarnation piece by piece.

These responses are not necessarily being chosen because they work in the moment; sometimes they do not work well at all, but they are part of the preexisting equipment. When a child appears to overreact to some minor situation, this may be due to the situation triggering a memory of a time long past, and the reaction is to that time rather than to the present. The personality is reflected in every part of the baby's world; the genes, the DNA, the lines of the palm, the surrounding people, and many other mirrors of life—and the birth chart maps the pattern of it all.

Looking at their child's birth chart can help parents be more understanding of the child's behavior. Children need to be the way they are, true to their feelings in the moment. They will benefit if we can help them use their set of characteristics with more awareness and skill; but if we try to change their basic character, we are simply burying the tools they need to fulfill their spirit's purpose. As parents, being part of the picture that will develop the child's character, we, too, need to be what we are to the best of our ability, accepting ourselves kindly, so that our children also learn to be accepting. In this way we can assist the unfolding of our children's potential in the best possible way.

Partnership

Another area of life where an informed look at birth charts can be helpful is partnership. All the individual people you relate to also have a birth chart; that is to say, their spirit chose a set of characteristics before coming to Earth. They, too, have an ideal to work toward, an aim to achieve, a purpose to discover, which may be very different from your own. Their survival behavior at birth would have been in accordance with their personality "tool kit," and their predisposition will have created their particular experiences and decisions about life. All these may not coincide with yours, even though you may be very attracted to them.

From the planetary positions at the time of a person's birth, we can see their chosen character and what their path through life may be about. Comparing your chart to their chart can indicate what connections there may be between you. The problems can be clearly seen, and therefore focused on in a constructive way. The chemistry of day-to-day living is complex and may seem insoluble unless we can step back into our "observer" mode and get a more detached look at what is going on. Astrology can provide that detached view.

Play with Astrology

The language of astrology is written in symbols. A symbol is like a doorway. Even within different philosophies, the meanings given to a very basic symbol will tend to be similar. Basic symbols are part of the structure of life itself, so quietly contemplating a symbol, or combination of symbols, can bring realizations about the aspect of life being represented.

All that is written about astrology is basically what different people have learned through contemplating and playing with astrological symbols and applying their learning to whatever area of life interests them, be it human character, world events, answers to questions, or the timing of events. If you would like to contemplate the symbols of astrology yourself, you will find that your understanding of the basic principles will be enhanced.

You can play with the ideas in astrology, just enjoying the astrological way of viewing life. It can be quite exciting to see, for the first time, which Zodiac sign Mercury was traveling through, or transiting, when you were born. At last, here is a reflection of the way your mind works and the kinds of things you communicate about most easily. The sign placement of Mercury can describe, among other things, why certain areas of experience fascinate you, while others do not interest you at all or may be difficult to understand. It also shows your particular needs in any learning situation.

Venus reflects the way we relate to people and the kind of surroundings we feel good in. Many of us tend to model our expectations of communication and relationship on the behavior accepted by society or our social group. This behavior may work for some people, but it is not nec-essarily the best way for everybody. Other people choose behavior out of *their* "tool kit"; ours may be very different. So, when we see which sign Venus was transiting at our birth, we may recognize at last that something personally important to us has been missing from our relationships. Ac-cepting that, we can start behaving in a way that will attract it into our re-lationships in the future.

When we examine our birth chart, the confirmation of our character and inner direction helps us release our potential. Accepting ourselves, we begin to hear, and give credence to, our own inner guidance.

If we could learn to accept ourselves totally and love all our experi-ence unconditionally, there would be no need for personal exploration of our makeup, our earthly equipment; we would blend with Oneness and the need for a personality would disappear. When we have difficulty with such complete acceptance, knowing how we function can help us under-stand and deal with the habitual pitfalls of our particular personality, and also help us believe in and use our finer qualities. Bringing assumptions and expectations into consciousness is the beginning of retrieving the power they seem to have over our behavior; we start to realize that we make our own lives, so we can choose to do things differently. This makes it easier for all of us to be the open, loving souls we truly are.

Our experience of life is what is true for us. A birth chart shows us a map of life experience, but not the experiences themselves. We get a more complete and detailed view of ourselves and what we are doing from what seems to be happening around us, reflecting us from many angles.

The usefulness of a birth chart depends on the quality of its interpre-tation; therefore, it should never be considered to be the last word in any situation. Before decisions are made in life, we need to look at the whole of our world, and also to look deep inside ourselves to the place of inner knowing.

Our chart may be able to suggest a meaning in events that helps us ac-cept them. It may offer us a direction in which to look, and help us recog-nize that the voice we hear is truly our own guidance, but it is not appro-priate to use astrology to make our decisions for us, nor to tell us what is the truth. Astrology itself can never give us the answers.

✿ ✿ One ✿ ✿

Philosophical Overview

The Center of the Circle

The symbol of the circle and cross is often used to represent healing. The unity of the circle and the harmony of the four equal arms represent the principle of total health on all levels.

We begin with a circle to represent all there is, all there can be, all potential, out of time. The point in the center of the circle symbolizes the point of creation where time begins— potential starts to become actual and there is separation. In astrology, the circle with a dot in the middle represents the Sun, the great light that hides the source of all life, the Sun itself being the creative source of light and life on Earth. If we extend the dot in the circle so that it becomes the two lines that divide the circle in half 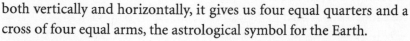 both vertically and horizontally, it gives us four equal quarters and a cross of four equal arms, the astrological symbol for the Earth.

The dot is where the two lines cross, and, when the four elements of manifested material life are balanced, that dot will be in the center of the circle. It is that center point that links us with the timelessness

9

of Unity: when we are balanced in ourselves, the Source is accessible to us, transforming our earthly experience with understanding and joy. To develop a powerful, effective, and happy state, we need to contact that center of our being, and there we can be in touch with our own innate wisdom and the essence of all life.

Astrology has the potential to help us reach that center point in ourselves. If we let the circle represent all astrological potential, we can divide it horizontally and vertically to find the center. Astrology can be divided into a science and an art, and also divided into its general use and personal use. First, we will divide the circle horizontally, one half illustrating its use at a general level, showing our *similarities* as human beings, and the other half showing its application on a personal level. At the personal level, individual birth charts are the tools that show our *differences* from each other.

We Are the Same, Only Different

There are many books and workshops to help us "peel the onion" of our personality to reach the center. Because they are structured for many people at the same time, they are generalized and based on our similarities. We are the same in that we are all human, we have parents, and we grow through childhood and adolescence and are subject to family and social conditioning. Each of us has a personality with many facets, and we share feelings with the same names, such as guilt, anger, and pleasure. Each of us also has the potential to reach that point within ourselves that feels like the truth of our center. Much of what is written and spoken about self-development addresses these similarities, with ideas such as taking responsibility for one's life, accepting people as they are, thinking positively to create positive experience, meditating to make contact with one's center, and so on. We all need these teachings, and working with others, all using the same method, helps give us a sense of our "oneness" with each other.

However, at a personality level, which is where we mostly live, we are very different from each other, and the methods of working with our own personal unfolding need to be as individual as we are ourselves. Every now and then in life, a person who is working toward a new, more aware style of life will need individual help, as they reach an unconscious attitude block or a repetitive behavioral plateau where the general words cannot be assimilated and used. They may work with a therapist of some kind or a friend, or may choose to work alone, but, without some sort of map as an unbiased overview, they can get lost. Astrology is a system as ancient as humanity that offers each individual a personal map. This map, or chart, is created mathematically from scientifically derived information based on the individual's time and place of birth. All this is as unbiased as one's reflection in a mirror. No judgment is offered by the chart, simply a statement of how it is.

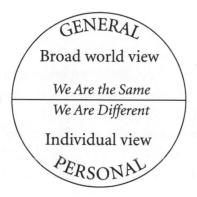

The branch of astrology that fascinates most people is natal astrology, that supremely personal view showing the reflection of *your* life on earth and *your* individual character, different from any other. Your birth chart reflects your personality with all its individuality and potential. It also shows the unconscious tendencies that may keep your potential from unfolding as fully as it could.

The interpretation of astrology that is not so often considered is the broader view, where we use the Zodiac signs, the celestial bodies, and the twelve divisions of the sky to describe the human condition in a *general* sense. Confusion can arise through the use of general astrology in newspapers and magazines, which is often written in more individualistic terms than is appropriate. This is a legitimate use of planets in Zodiac signs, but can be misleading when it is taken too personally.

The general view describes the whole of human potential; each person is capable of expressing qualities of all the Zodiac signs, and everyone's life force has all the functions represented by all the planets. The most complete reflection of humanity as a whole, and even of one individual person, is the entire sky. If we want to see a reflection of our individual selves, we have only to look at the night sky with all its wonders. Even then, all that we can see on a clear night is only half of our reflection, the other half being beneath the earth.

It is good to remember that we help ourselves evolve not only by learning to accept our particular reflection in our birth chart, but also by learning to accept other people as reflected in their birth charts. We also evolve by recognizing how we are all little splinters of the great human hologram, described in "The Zodiac Story" in chapter 2. Each one of us contains the whole human experience, and each one of us is also individually expressed by the whole; that is to say, "I *am* all of it," and also, "It all reflects me."

We are all human beings, different because of our individual perceptions of life; and each one of us, as part of Oneness, is also a doorway for the expression of all creation. Bearing this in mind, we recognize the need to balance the two halves of the circle and align ourselves with the line across the center.

Logic and Intuition

We can also divide the astrological circle vertically, the scientific method on the left, and the art of practice on the right.

The science of astrology takes the movements of stars and planets, from the point of view of the Earth, drawn as a two-dimensional pattern, and describes them using the principles and meanings laid down over centuries of experience. In natal astrology, this drawing is a chart, or picture, of the time and place of birth of a character, and the description is a character analysis, which can be run off a computer. If the information built into the program is accurate and well expressed, a printout for a particular birth time will be a good analysis.

The art of astrology is the intuitive blending, or synthesis, of the astrological principles involved in a chart, in order to interpret that chart for its owner in a helpful and appropriate way. Even people with almost identical charts can receive individual readings relevant to their experiences and that address the roots of their beliefs about life. This kind of chart reading involves an intuitive rapport with clients in order to describe the chart in a way they recognize as themselves.

Such a chart reading will confirm people's experiences of themselves and their lives. It will show them how it is possible to create more enjoyable experiences at work, in relationships, and so on. It will give them a more conscious sense of their own potential as being achievable, and a feeling that they are valuable and worthy of self-acceptance. A good reading will enable people to align with their most satisfying course of action, and will suggest what would feel good to focus on next.

The science of astrology requires use of the left brain, while the art of astrology is an expression of the right brain. Without the art of astrology, one can be an expert in the science of astrology, yet give a useless and even damaging interpretation of a birth chart. On the other hand, without an accurate chart, even practicing the art of astrology in a healing way will still give false information. What is needed is a balance between the two sides to align ourselves with the line down the center.

Astrology as a Guide to the Center Point

In a chart reading, the astrologer needs to help clients balance the way they see themselves, both as individuals (their differences) and as people in relationship with the rest of humanity (their similarities with others), so that their personal development will not cut them off from society. This balancing also allows each individual's growth and greater awareness to "salt the pot" of humanity, because every individual development, however apparently small, is reflected in the whole.

In each of the following chapters, this first division of the circle will be made by talking about the general meaning of the astrological principles in a first section

Place of transformation

called "Ways in Which We Are the Same," followed by a second section called "Ways in Which We Are Different," containing the particular, individual use of these principles for personal understanding, relationship, and growth.

When we use scientifically calculated birth charts and the ancient principles of astrology, and practice the interpretation of them as an art, we strengthen the link between the two hemispheres of the brain. This second division of the circle will be made clear by the words themselves speaking sequentially to the left brain, and the symbols and many of the ideas speaking to the right brain. Shifting ideas from left-brain words to right-brain understanding, and back, can be facilitated by carrying out the exercises given throughout this book.

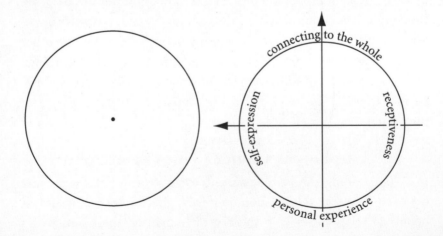

connecting to the whole

self-expression

receptiveness

Personal experience

To be on both dividing lines at once puts us on the dot in the center of the circle, the hole in the middle where we can fall through the center of our being into All That Is. Enabling people to get to that place in themselves allows a transformative experience to occur in a chart reading. When we read a chart well, we are combining the intellectual and intuitive faculties of the brain and expressing them through the heart.

From the spirit symbol of the Sun, the dot within the circle, we have arrived at the Earth symbol, the circle and cross, which is the shape of the astrological birth chart itself. The chart shows how we balance our personal experience (below the horizon) with our connection to the whole (above the horizon), and our self-expression (left side) with our receptiveness (right side). All this is contained within the circle of Zodiac signs and houses, which express all potential human experience.

Astrology in a Nutshell

An **astrological birth chart** consists of the following:

1. The **planets**, which represent *life energy* flowing through us with different functions.

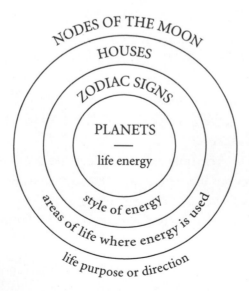

2. The **Zodiac signs**, which indicate the *style* or *manner* in which each energy (planet) is expressed.

3. The **houses** where the planets are located, which describe the *areas of our life* that encourage us to use that energy, and the activities that get the energy going.

4. The planets are said to be in relationship with each other when the number of degrees between them is significant. **Aspects** is the name given to planetary relationships, each of a specific number of degrees indicating a different reaction between them. I generally use only numbers that are multiples of 30°, thereby keeping the scientific side simple. Thus there are six aspects, including the conjunction, and each one describes a different relationship between the two planets involved.

5. Basically, this is all that needs to be known, but I like to include the **Nodes of the Moon**, which suggest our most satisfying life direction and how to achieve it. I use this lunar axis because finding a direction or purpose for this life can integrate all the other factors in the chart, and thus help us integrate our divergent personality traits. It creates a life "story" that feels right and satisfying, and helps us accept ourselves.

A typical birth chart is shown on the next page. It shows the horizon at the time of birth across the middle, and the due south/north line labeled "MC" at the top, which together create the four quadrants and thus the twelve numbered houses. The planets are shown in the signs they occupied at birth. Their geometrical relationships, experienced as innate personality reactions, are indicated by the lines connecting them with each other. The points called the Nodes of the Moon are opposite each other.

It is crucial to remember that astrology neither makes us who we are, nor creates our life experience. The birth chart describes us, as a map describes a landscape or a mirror reflects a face. Our personality is our spirit's choice, and what we do in our life is up to us.

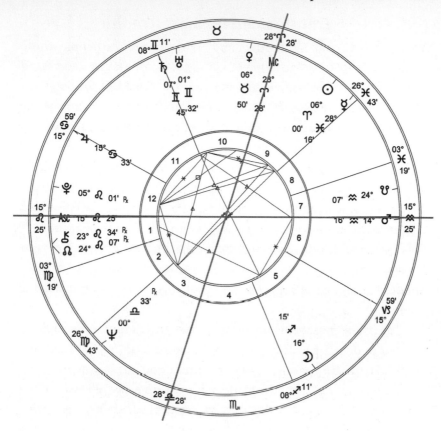

Transformative Chart Reading

We need to be gentle, accepting, and loving toward the people whose birth charts we read, including ourselves. It is not easy to understand our own chart because we have so much assumed "knowledge" of ourselves; so, if we begin by imagining our unknown self sitting beside us, it will be easier to create an attitude of really wanting to know this self better.

When reading a birth chart, we need to work within two beliefs: first, that each person's life can be meaningful; and second, that experience is useful when we learn something positive from it. The added sense that life itself is a joy, combined with a love of people as individuals, will make your time together a healing experience for your clients, regardless of how much or how little astrological knowledge you have. This helps people be open to change and growth during the reading.

One of the most valuable results of a chart reading is the ability it gives us to detach a little from our personality, enabling us to see ourselves. At the beginning of your readings, you may want to spend some time talking about the planets in signs on a casual level, so that clients can start to look at themselves in this detached way, even seeing where in the chart their characteristics are reflected.

Then you will need to focus on the places where clients are having trouble in life, giving away their power to situations or other people. These painful areas will be shown by planetary principles that are in an uncomfortable position in the chart, and clients are likely to want to reject those experiences. Since the whole chart is always in operation, the rejected energies do not disappear, but will instead be reflected by the behavior of relatives, colleagues, and bosses, and difficulties will show up in relationship with those people. So we describe the characteristic that is being projected onto others by describing the relevant planet in its sign and house.

It is a good idea, when searching for a way to describe a particular planet in a chart, first to give clients an idea of what it might feel like, and then have them describe in their own words how it feels to them and what actually seems to happen in that area of life. You might also ask them why they feel the need or desire to judge and reject a particular feeling or behavior, in order to discover what their difficulty is with handling that energy. Individuals are far more complex than the few celestial details we put in a chart, and an astrologer can learn something new with every reading.

At this point in a reading, depending on your counseling abilities, it may be relevant to speak of the early life where the difficulties appear to have begun. It is best to avoid *blaming* parents because this perpetuates a sense of being a victim. So together you might even create images of possible past lives, because earlier experiences could be replaying in this lifetime. It is not important to be "accurate" about past lives. The crucial factor is whether it "feels right" to the recipient.

Using past lives as a description of origins of reactions and behavior is useful in that it takes the fear we have of people and events away from the future, and places it in the past in a time that was very different from this lifetime. The feared event has already happened and what we have now is only the memory of the trauma. It may be that the person we have been reacting to recently merely reminds us of someone we tangled with painfully in the past.

Once we realize that it is our fear and expectation of remembered events that has been recreating our experiences, we are free to let go of the expectation. By understanding that our reactions probably have a good cause, we can more easily accept our pain.

Using your knowledge of astrological meanings, however small you feel it to be, you can, at this point, show how the rejected energy could manifest if it were expressed in more positive ways, and what abilities it might indicate. As clients accept the energy in that form, they begin to feel it in themselves. They find both that this energy feels natural to them, and also that the ability that goes with it is something they already do in certain circumstances with positive results.

As clients integrate the idea of these characteristics, it becomes possible to describe their potential, shown by the rest of the chart, in terms that they feel is actually possible to achieve. The order of the chart reading does not have to be as stated here. The best guides are the way the conversation goes with the recipient, and your own intuition. Many negatively experienced issues may arise during a reading, requiring positive and useful vision to balance them. The truth is that every ability needs to be used with care, and every difficulty teaches a skill. If we cannot find the balancing vision, trusting that it exists will be enough to keep us steady.

In the following chapters, the Zodiac signs, planets, and houses are expressed in ways that will give you the sense of a complete picture, enabling chart readings to be transformative experiences.

The recipients of such a reading will be unfolding inside while the reading proceeds; during the process, changes will be occurring in their mental structuring, and their programmed beliefs and expectations. Because of these developments, changes will also be occurring in the emotions. Sometimes clients will shift position suddenly, sigh deeply, cry, or laugh, all of which indicate an internal shift. Through these emotional and bodily changes, the hormones, the glands that secrete them, and the whole energy system of the body are undergoing a shakeup, a healing.

This ultimately affects the basic life programming in the genes and DNA because the physical body is structured according to the energy system. People are brought into the present time at a very deep level through the acceptance of who they really are—the transformation. It can be likened to developmental homeopathy; the potency of the remedy in a transformative chart reading is the vibrational sound of the spoken word accurately prescribed.

As the genes are affected, what was hereditary is changed for future generations. It is not necessary to pass on to our children everything that has come down from our ancestors. Changing the structure of bodies being born, through releasing restrictive belief patterns, enables finer, wiser spirits to incarnate without getting lost in the negative programming of our present world. We need them!

✿ ✿ Two ✿ ✿

The Zodiac

Ways in Which We Are the Same

The Four Elements

The system of four elements is an ancient way of describing All That Is. The idea is that everything is composed of a combination of four "elements": earth and water, air and fire, like the building blocks of DNA.

There is a generic chant:

"Earth is my body, Water, my blood,
Air is my breath, and Fire, my spirit."

Added together, the four elements create "ether," or life force. Their perfect balance in an individual person shows as physical, emotional, and mental health, combined with personal spiritual contact.

Each element has three qualities, or ways of being. *Cardinal* is pushes outward, *fixed* is within itself, and *mutable* is changeable.

⬆ An element in its **cardinal** state *expresses* toward the world.

⬛ An element in its **fixed** state *is* in its own being.

〰 An element in its **mutable** state *adapts* to circumstances and pressure.

Imagine each of the four elements drawn as a triangle, with its three points representing the qualities of cardinal, fixed, and mutable.

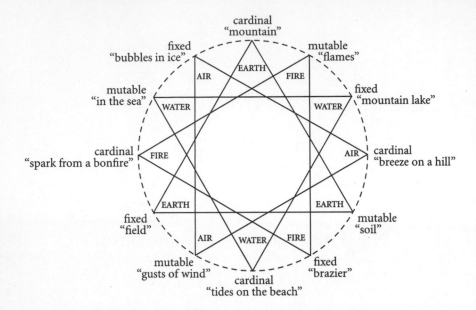

Evenly placed in a circle, these four triangles make twelve points on the circumference, which link in with the twelve Zodiac signs.

Each element has a meaning in terms of personality traits, and in the following table, words are grouped according to those meanings. Each quality, each of the three ways of being an element, has been given an image in this table, to assist the intuitive, conceptual side of the brain to join in the quest for understanding. Those images are expanded in "The Zodiac Story" later in this chapter. Eventually, by allowing all the symbols to trigger understanding, each Zodiac symbol will become a key to the door of one of the twelve signs. Open the door with that key and your intuition can enter into one-twelfth of All That Is.

FIRE—The realm of transformation. Fire can be enthusiastic, loving, affectionate, and warm. It can also be fanatical or idealistic, destructive or creative with life energy, angry and passionate, and it needs fuel.

Cardinal—Aries—"spark from a bonfire"

Fixed—Leo—"brazier"

Mutable—Sagittarius—"flames"

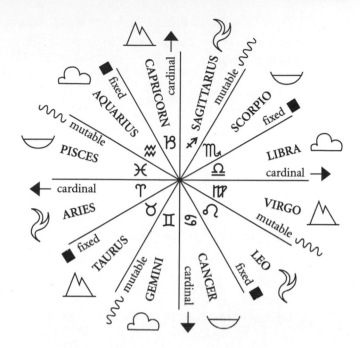

AIR—The realm of thought and ideas. Air has clarity, fast movement, speech, logic, and elegance. Sometimes it can be cold and unfeeling, using logic over common sense, and it needs freedom.

- Cardinal—Libra—"breeze on a hill"

- Fixed—Aquarius—"bubbles in ice"

- Mutable—Gemini—"gusts of wind"

WATER—The realm of emotion and psychic experience. Water is irrational, cleansing, flowing, sensitive, and gentle, the nurturing womb. It can be overwhelming, pressuring or flooding, and it needs movement.

- Cardinal—Cancer—"tides on the beach"

- Fixed—Scorpio—"mountain lake"

- Mutable—Pisces—"in the sea"

EARTH—The realm of material effect. Earth is practical, heavy, slow, sensible, serious, supportive, and nourishing. It can be stuck, rigid, depressed, and it needs time.

↑ Cardinal—Capricorn—*"mountain"*

■ Fixed—Taurus—*"field"*

〰 Mutable—Virgo—*"soil"*

EXERCISES

1. Meditate on each element as three images, noticing the different qualities each image expresses.

2. Choose other images to express the different qualities of each element.

The Zodiac Signs as Twelve Pieces of a Process

Just for a moment, see each activity you do as the process of cutting a round cake. Choose a place to begin and cut the cake into twelve slices. To begin cutting the first slice, you need the courage to take a step where no one else has gone before. Aries is about beginnings: it is open, fresh, ready to start something new, full of energy, and impatient to see results. The other eleven slices will be cut in order around the cake until you reach the twelfth slice, which, like Pisces, completes the "disintegration" of the whole cake into parts.

Each of the twelve signs in the Zodiac has a specific meaning that relates to its place in the process, from Aries at the beginning, to Pisces, the twelfth and last sign.

You could have cut the cake into a different number of slices, say thirteen or ten, but each slice would then be a different size; that is to say, the meaning of each piece in terms of its part in the process would be a bit different. If you divide anything into pieces, then every piece is needed to make the thing whole.

The Zodiac Signs as Twelve Seasons in a Cycle

The cycle of the natural seasons can be compared to the cycle of the Zodiac. This is because the qualities of each season match those of the signs containing the Sun at that time of year. The cycle is divided into four seasons: spring, summer, autumn, and winter, each with its cardinal sign stating its beginning, its fixed sign sure of the season's identity in the middle, and its mutable sign transforming into the following season.

1. Aries ♈—*Cardinal spring*. The energy bursting out of the ground as though impatient from having been confined by the cold; new plans for the year. Starts at the spring equinox, around March 21.

2. Taurus ♉—*Fixed spring*. We become used to the sense of growth with fresh, new green everywhere; the Maypole comes out; the bull reminds us of fertility rites.

3. Gemini ♊—*Mutable spring*. The gusty winds are friendly and promise warmth not yet to be trusted; preparing for the summer.

4. Cancer ♋—*Cardinal summer.* The summer solstice, around June 21; it is the time of rising energy, of maximum growth; the Earth nurturing all her children.

5. Leo ♌—*Fixed summer.* We have come to expect hot days; leaves have been around long enough to be dusty; children are on holiday from school, having fun.

6. Virgo ♍—*Mutable summer.* The leaves are starting to change color and we notice the days getting shorter; we have the sense that the fruits will not be there forever, and we begin the labor of the harvest.

7. Libra ♎—*Cardinal autumn.* Having gratefully harvested the fruits of our labor, at the autumn equinox, around September 23, we give in order to balance what we have been given.

8. Scorpio ♏—*Fixed autumn.* It becomes clear that we must get ready for the coming cold, preparing to protect ourselves; chill and damp; Halloween and fireworks around the bonfire in the dark.

9. Sagittarius ♐—*Mutable autumn.* We have our warmer clothes on now, preparing for Christmas; lights, during the longer evenings we gather around the fire to pass the time.

10. Capricorn ♑—*Cardinal winter.* The winter solstice, around December 21, marks the power underground, the plentiful food and gifts at Christmas supplied by one who has either worked for it, or who has it by inheritance.

11. Aquarius ♒—*Fixed winter.* The cold has set in, ice and snow, and the ground is so hard that nothing can get through except the snowdrop; a vision of perfect purity.

12. Pisces ♓—*Mutable winter.* The ice begins to melt and more flowers bloom, but the cold keeps returning; change is in the air; who knows what the coming year will bring?

Seasons are different in every country, but the cycle of beginning, growth, maturing, digesting, dispersion, and new beginning is the cycle of life itself. If any piece of this process is left out, the rest of the process cannot happen.

The Zodiac Signs as Twelve Pieces of a Personality

As it is with the Zodiac as a process, so it is when the Zodiac is used to describe the personality: if any sign is removed, the personality will not be complete. We each need to have the qualities of every Zodiac sign in order to be a whole person.

We all have every Zodiac sign in our personality somewhere, so it is very important to be able to see the best side of each sign as well as its problems. Sometimes people talk about one sign or another as though life would be better without it, but this would make life incomplete. If we can learn to use the best of each sign, we will be honest, useful, happy, and fully rounded people. Also, we will be able to understand other people much better and recognize what is valuable in them, no matter what sign they are.

Learning to express love through each of the twelve signs is a way to become aware of our Godself, the highest expression of our center. It is like the twelve disciples, who together in spirit reflect Jesus, or twelve consecutive semitones on a piano in sound that span an octave: each one of the twelve is an individual expression of one part of the essence, which has twelve aspects.

The following is a list of all the Zodiac signs and the pieces of our personality that they reflect. Some of them will be familiar—pieces you know that you have. Others might be pieces you admire in other people, and there may be one or two that you have never thought about.

The words in quotation marks and parentheses are picture images that express some of the essence of the sign. The bold-type word is a quality of each sign that can help us enjoy life and be valuable people. The italicized sentences suggest a focus that can assist in developing the bolded quality.

Listed under each sign are some activities in which the abilities of the sign would be useful, although most activities require the abilities of more than one sign.

Aries ♈ ("spark from a bonfire")—**Courageous,** new beginnings, fresh, ready to start something new, full of energy, impatient to see results, ready to attack rather than be frustrated or stuck, can be aggressive. Useful when starting something new, and also when self-motivation is required.

Learning to use the right amount of energy for each situation.

Taurus ♉ ("field")—**Grounded, dependable,** practical, earthy, helping people to be healthy by sharing earth energy, slow, quiet, concerned about security, can be stubborn and unchanging. Useful in gardening, cooking, etc., and when others need steady support.

Learning to make peaceful contact with nature.

Gemini ♊ ("gusts of wind")—**Able to talk with anyone,** finding out things and telling people, imagining or thinking things out, at least two of everything, sometimes charming, sometimes silent, alternating between two personalities, two homes, two jobs, can be unreliable. Useful when needing information, putting people at ease, or writing.

Learning to use both sides of the brain—balancing intuition and logic.

Cancer ♋ ("tides on the beach")—**Emotionally sensitive,** up-and-down moods, family loving, half childish and half like a loving parent, caring or needing to be cared for, nurturing, can hold on to people too tightly. Useful when homemaking, empathizing with a friend, or giving quality time to young children.

Learning to be steady and supportive in emotional situations.

Leo ♌ ("brazier")—**Open-hearted,** loving, dramatic, encouraging, enjoys leading or entertaining other people, proud of one's self, sunny, can be too loud and pushy, pride can be easily hurt. Useful at parties, when others are feeling down, or when giving a talk or teaching.

Learning to stay loving and positive no matter what other people think.

Virgo ♍ ("soil")—**Making things better,** helpful, aiming for perfection, efficient, wanting to be right, can be critical, self-critical, or fussy. Useful when putting things in order, making things carefully, or sorting out what is important.

> *Learning to accept things and people as they are,*
> *as a basis for improving life.*

Libra ♎ ("breeze on a hill")—**Diplomatic,** relating to others pleasantly, balancing self-interest with interest in other people, peacemaking, supporting the underdog, listening to all sides of an argument, can be hesitant for fear of spoiling things. Useful in meetings, or when choosing colors, clothes, or decor.

> *Learning to gather all the information necessary*
> *to make the correct decision.*

Scorpio ♏ ("mountain lake")—**Emotional understanding,** feeling things deeply, strong, knowing about the difficult side of life, wanting to know what is going on under the surface, intense, can be unkind and want revenge. Useful when you need to be determined, or for understanding deep hurt in others.

> *Learning to use painful times for growth and understanding.*

Sagittarius ♐ ("flames")—**Enthusiastic, optimistic,** always seeing the positive possibilities, interested in everything, full of fun, enjoying discussions about life, traveling, teaching, exploring, can rush about or fail to explain what you mean clearly. Useful when enthusiasm is needed.

> *Learning to share your interests so that other people*
> *can expand their thinking.*

Capricorn ♑ ("mountain")—**Working to get what you want,** doing your best, careful, results more important than feelings, strong and reliable, sometimes assumes too much responsibility, can be too serious or bossy. Useful for organizing other people, or when figuring out how to do something practical.

> *Learning to reach what you decide you want*
> *by using intention rather than heavy labor.*

Aquarius ♒ ("bubbles in ice")—**Having an overview,** seeing the best way to organize people, knowing what will work, wanting equal opportunities for everyone, feeling free, observing people, can seem cold and unfriendly. Useful when others panic, or when you're on your own.

> *Learning that everyone has something to give, and that although people*
> *are equal in value they are not all the same.*

Pisces ♓ ("in the sea")—**Putting other people first,** knowing that you are really a light spirit in an earthly body, very emotional, feeling everybody's feelings, wanting to help everybody feel better, sometimes feeling resentful, forgetting to ask for help. Useful when meditating, or in counseling.

> *Learning to be in touch with spirit joy so that it can be shared*
> *with everyone you meet.*

EXERCISES

1. All activities require the abilities of one or more signs—think of things that you do, and figure out which signs you need to do them well.

2. If you know your chart, see if you have any planetary energy in these particular signs.

3. Whether you know your chart or not, try to express these signs to the best of your ability when engaged in these activities.

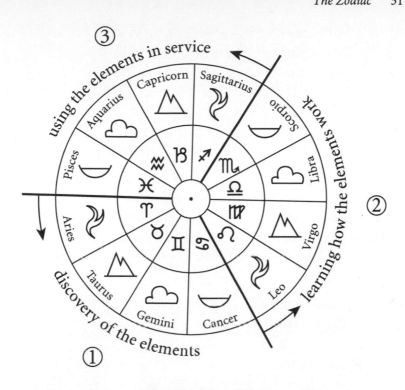

The Zodiac Story

The meaning of the Zodiac is inherent in creation because it describes any cyclic process. I like describing the Zodiac as the process of a spirit evolving a clear and complete human character through experience on Earth. It is our own story. Each sign can be said to represent a stage of life, a quality of experience, a way of feeling in relation to the world; and each one of us experiences all the signs as we go through life.

Let us imagine, insofar as we are able, the all-inclusive Oneness becoming the Source of all life, which proceeds to extend its divine fire. The extensions feel individual (Aries) and make the original error of thinking that they are separate from their Source. These individual sparks, or spirits, manifest surroundings (Taurus) to push against in order to become aware, understanding, and effective in the same way as their creator. The surroundings are earth, the focus of experience, and the Zodiac describes that experience as twelve lessons expressing growth. In this story, the perfect growth of the spirit through one round of the Zodiac signs creates the perfect human archetype through which the spirit becomes aware again of its Oneness with the Source (Pisces).

The movement through the signs can be seen as breathing. The out-breaths are in fire and air; the in-breaths are in earth and water. This makes the pattern of out–fire, in–earth, out–air, in–water, repeated twice more, making six great breaths in all. Now let us tell the story of this great life development.

a spark of life, tiny but hugely bright, brave, with no thought for the future,
catching the eye for a moment, inspiring hope

Aries ♈
"spark from a bonfire"

At first there was only the sea of unified unconsciousness, and, in a moment, one drop of that ocean used its energy to leap out of the waves into free space. This is the experience of Aries, this first thought that, because there is a self, then the rest of existence is separate. The energy is powerful and drives the spirit forward to discover what this "self" is like.

In the Aries character you find a wonder about life, an ability to be amazed as though this is their first view of the world. This drive to discover can sometimes knock other people flat with its naive exuberance.

Aries energy is often experienced by others as aggressive and combative, and certainly competitive, but this can be due to the vague fear of disappearing back into the oblivion experienced in Pisces. The competitiveness is needed to discover the limits of the newly found self, rather than to have power over another. The combativeness in the face of perceived blocks is due to the buildup of life energy that is being frustrated.

If weapons are taken up against an Aries, their confident stance dissolves, and what appears to be selfishness is due to thoughtlessness and a lack of understanding of other people's needs. All can be remedied with explanation and discussion—after all, Aries rules the head: the ventricles of the brain are shaped like ram's horns, the ram being the Aries symbol.

In Aries, the spirit learns to let raw energy flow through, giving life to its own and other people's ideas, starting projects and always moving on to new realms. It is the discovery of fire, the element that represents energy and expresses itself through activity, humor, and affection. Later, in Leo, the second fire sign, controlling fire has priority, and in Sagittarius, the third and last fire sign, fire needs to be used constructively.

*a field, secure delicious pasture, meadow flowers in the sun,
breathing sweet and lazy warmth*

Taurus ♉
"field"

Having developed consciousness of individuality and an energetic drive, the spirit is ready to gather a physical manifestation around itself. The sign of Taurus is the first contact with earth, and the earth force flows freely through a Taurus character, spreading a relaxing atmosphere toward whoever is around. For this reason, Taurus people are the natural physical healers of the Zodiac, needing only to contact another person with their hands, with a pat on the back or a brief cuddle, to create a sense of harmony and physical well-being in the other. At its most powerful, that touch can remove blockages in a person's energy flow and heal the body.

The earth element represents the material world and expresses itself through stability, solidity, and dependability. The symbol of Taurus is the bull. We most often think of a bull in its own field, perhaps with a cow around for his natural gratification. It is as though he owns his patch, and the world can do as it likes outside the fence.

The bull's anger is aroused only by trespassers or anyone else who attempts to steal what Taurus regards as his own, but as soon as his furious charge has ejected the trespasser, and the stolen possessions are returned to him, Taurus' anger dissolves.

It is the fertility of the bull that signifies Taurus, its slowness to begin movement and its contentment with worldly pleasures. In the Taurus character this can manifest as a stubborn, stick-in-the-mud attitude or laziness, but there is a fear of insecurity, not knowing what is going on outside the fence or how they will survive if things change. When Taurus people are in any way upset or suffering, contact with nature will heal them.

In Taurus, the spirit learns about the flow of earth energy, the limits of the body and its energy, and the extent of physical needs. In the second earth sign, Virgo, the lesson is how the material world works, and in Capricorn, the third and last earth sign, this knowledge is applied for the benefit of the world at large.

*gusts of wind whirling flashes of news around and letting go to play
with leaves, dancing with us and then gone*

Gemini ♊
"gusts of wind"

With consciousness of itself and the ability to gather a physical form,
the spirit is now ready to explore mentally everything that it sees as
not itself, through Gemini. This is the spirit's first contact with air, the
element that represents the world of ideas. Air expresses itself through
thought and the communication of that thought. The Gemini mind
goes out looking for ideas and things in order to understand them
sufficiently to name them and then to communicate that understanding to others.

It is not necessary for Gemini to understand deeply or to study a
subject for a long time. The speedy grasp of essentials is all that is required to pass on the information and then move on to something
else. It is not even necessary that the information should add up to
make a larger picture; that will be the task in Sagittarius. For Gemini,
such adding together would take time they would rather spend finding more information. This can look like a butterfly mind, always
touching ideas but never going deep enough to see where they lead.
But the communication of these ideas to the public is invaluable, and

the Gemini character has already developed the ability to communicate with anyone. Their interest, combined with flexibility of expression, gives them the knack of charming all kinds of people into conversation, and the versatility of their mind is well suited to learning anybody's language. On the other hand, the need to communicate can lead to empty chatter that is difficult to stop.

The symbol of Gemini is the twins, a symbol of duality, perhaps the two sides of the brain: the left hemisphere having the ability to think logically and make words and sentences, and the right hemisphere housing the ability to understand at a glance, to intuit, to imagine. In Gemini behavior, there often appears to be two characters within one person, one outward and communicative, the other a mystery, sometimes silent, or even depressed or morose.

Perhaps the secret of this dual personality rests in the blending of the two hemispheres of the brain. The silent half may need to communicate the imaginative side through creativity, without words. Whatever the solution, it can be witnessed that Gemini people usually prefer to have at least two of everything, maybe to express their own inner differences.

In Gemini, the spirit flexes its mental muscles in order to build a clever and versatile brain, capable of questing far into the universe along logically constructed bridges, a truly wonderful tool. In the second air sign, Libra, that tool is used to explore relationships between people, and in the third and last air sign, Aquarius, the vision thus acquired is applied to the organization of society as a whole.

tide advancing slowly closer and closer, wets our feet with salt,
ebbing away before coming closer again

Cancer ♋

"tides on a beach"

At last the spirit is ready for its baptism in water, the last of the four elements in this sequence. Water, as an element in astrology, represents the world of emotion, the psychic world. The symbol of Cancer is said negatively to represent the claws of a crab. Positively it shows the arms and breasts of the mother. Cancer is the sign of mother and child, enfolded so closely that they dream as one and live emotionally blended. The relationship begins in the womb, and so we could say that the spirit in Cancer draws its earthly material into the form of a fetus surrounded by the waters of the chosen mother's womb.

The mother is chosen in the sense that each spirit requires the genes and upbringing that will create the personality to be worked with in the coming life. This personality will be a blend of some of those difficulties that still have to be smoothed out from previous earthly encounters, together with the abilities that are necessary to achieve that smoothing out and move the spirit further along the road to fulfillment.

The element of water expresses itself through feeling. Like water, the sea of emotion surrounds all of us all the time, and fills, as it were, the psychic space between us, enabling us to register the feelings of another. The Cancer character experiences this psychic sea of emotion as waves of contentment or sadness or resentment or hilarity, like moods over which there is no control. These moods come and go like waves on the beach, like the tides, high and low and high again. There is no sense of a need to control these moods: "If I am low today, to-morrow my mood may be high again, or if not tomorrow, then the next day." A feeling of anger will be contained and lived with, but, of course, those living around the Cancer person will feel the anger fill the room. Likewise, the hilarity is infectious, and the contentment is warming.

Cancer reaches out to people emotionally to care for, to nurture, to mother, and often to receive all those things from another. To feel and to give the security of mother-love is a strong need. With such a need, the Cancer person is emotionally dependent on the one who is fulfill-ing the other side of the bond, whether "child" or "mother." This is where the clingy nature of the crab is seen, and it tells us that only half the person is awake.

The real need is for Cancer people to mother their own inner child so that they don't present a vacuum, a neediness of love, to the world. One way to do this is to imagine the child as a separate form. Each time the feelings of neediness for another person come up, those feel-ings can then be looked at as belonging to this imaginary child. Then we know what to do to help the child feel better: we would naturally hold and love a child in such distress.

So we love and cuddle the imaginary child, and the sense of need-iness is forgotten and eventually healed. Taking this child everywhere we go, our inner neediness begins to trust the adult we have become, and there will be a time when that child disappears because it has been reintegrated into the adult self.

From the security this gives, Cancer people are then able to give the love freely to others, not holding on to them when nurturing is no longer necessary, able to let their children come and go without strings attached. Mothering the inner child requires an attitude of gentle acceptance of everything expressed without judging it to be good or bad. When we judge our inner child, we freeze our growth with fear of disapproval and rejection.

Any emotion we feel may once have been an essential reaction to a survival issue. We needed to feel the way we did. The only judgment of any value is whether or not the emotion is appropriate to the present moment. If we say the emotion is wrong, we freeze inside. If we can say, "In what situation was this emotion appropriate?" and allow ourselves not to be wrong about that, then we can look again at the present moment and see it more clearly as it is. In this way the inner child grows up gradually, and we become more able to relate to situations and people as they really are.

In Cancer, the spirit learns that although the emotions change, swell, and fade like the Moon in its phases or the tides on the beach, there is a stable center that is not affected by the surrounding conditions. The Moon is a globe and only its appearance changes. The sea is a stable quantity of water, and only the very edges of its shape move a little, shifting its emphasis in one direction or another in accordance with the Moon. Identifying with that stable center requires a trust that the Great World Mother will nourish us if we participate in her work of loving and caring for humanity in all its growing phases.

In Cancer, the spirit learns to relax in the process of changing and in the face of powerful emotions, secure in the knowledge that life itself is creative and will always nurture us with its abundance. The second water sign, Scorpio, explores the emotional aspect of relationships with others, and tries different ways to protect its own vulnerability. Pisces, the third and last water sign, uses the accumulated sensitivity about feelings to serve all people and to try to make the world a better place.

warm in the chilly evening, roasting nuts to share, heat from inside attracts a cozy group, don't put it out!

Leo ♌
"brazier"

The spirit now learns to steer clear of dependence on others, and to identify itself as an individual in the same way it did in Aries, but now it can begin to use the fire of that drive to affect its surroundings. This stage in growth can be likened to the little child who is old enough to sit and smile and give her imperious directions to doting admirers. All that is needed is that the admirers know the child's desires, and then those desires are fulfilled—as long as the child can express the desires in an effective way. The question is how to communicate effectively.

Usually a radiant smile is enough, but sometimes it may be necessary to resort to shouts and even a powerful use of emotional force. The Leo character becomes adept at handling whichever method works—unless the family is not admiring of the radiation at all. Then the child will learn that radiating is not effective in survival and the result is a person who retires and is quiet and sad. The shoulders may be rounded, protecting the damaged heart center of the body. There is no joy here.

We need to know that when the spirit expresses itself through Leo, radiation is the only means of communication that it has. Learning how to communicate without blasting other people is difficult. If that radiation is unacceptable, there is a complete loss of confidence and a collapse of the ego. When ridiculed or criticized, that powerful presence can be seen to be the paper-thin protection of a child in need of constant encouragement. Radiation requires an enormous amount of energy, and when Leos are ill or recovering from a setback, they will often hide from even their closest friends to lick their wounds in peace. It is as though they cannot bear to be with people unless they can radiate.

Another difficulty that Leos experience is that of receiving feedback from their "audience." Radiating is an outflow, and the more energy Leo people feel they must put in to keep the outflow going, the less they are able to feel the response of the person they are flowing toward. So they are very likely to overdo the outflow by talking too much, laughing too hard, or forgetting to listen. But in spite of all this, who does not smile back at the warmth, tolerate the pressure, and enjoy the love and laughter in the true Leo humor? Only people who are wrapped up in their own problems and need to "have their turn"—or another Leo perhaps!

In Leo, the spirit builds the courage to be like the Sun and radiate regardless of the likes or dislikes of the surrounding people, and also radiates only what is appropriate for the life of those surroundings. It is necessary to have courage to wield the fire that gives warmth, that gives life and love, but it must be blended with observation and sensitivity in order not to burn those who are loved.

crumbling earthy potential growth, clay, potential pots for use;
earth's voice in tiny insect sounds, busy

Virgo ♍
"soil"

Let's imagine the child a little older now, old enough to crawl about, getting into all the cupboards and pulling things out; and also old enough to walk and reach things above the head, including pan handles on the stove. Curiosity motivates an exploration of the physical world: What is it like? How does it fit together? What is it made of? How much pressure will it take? The exploration is of a mental nature, questioning, examining, all with the ultimate view of improving things, sometimes creating quite a mess in the initial process!

The Virgo character is adept at spotting flaws and pointing them out so that they can be corrected. However, most of the Zodiac signs are fairly content to leave the material world as it is, and the perfectionistic Virgo is often accused of constant hair-splitting, nit-picking, and criticizing. Virgo people can feel as though they have a mission to tell the truth as they see it and thereby improve all things to maximum efficiency so that there is no waste. We could all do with a bit more of this characteristic for the sake of our health and a balanced ecology, but it is exacting and often thankless work, and Virgos can easily feel overburdened and misunderstood.

The worst of it is that Virgo's own actions and personality get inner criticism first. They are the ones who suffer most at their own hands. They can suffer from a constant inner nagging voice, correcting and complaining how they *never* get it right and *always* make mistakes, because they feel that they should be perfect. Other people's complaints simply confirm their view of their own imperfection.

The mistake that the Virgo character tends to make is to think that perfection is something that can be achieved in the material world, that results should be perfect. They have an image of what perfection in a future situation would look like, but it is impossible to know what is perfectly appropriate until that moment in the future has become the present. The perfection we need to aim for is in the doing: It is possible for us to do our best, and that is perfect effort, moving with our sense of rightness as we go along. The results we get, no matter how we acted, perfectly serve to show us the style of our doing. So, as we grow, we can learn to improve our way of doing things. The necessary qualities of acute, conscious focus and the ability to discriminate are part of the Virgo personality.

Sometimes Virgo people forget to take into account a person's emotional state, level of maturity, and even bodily limitations, so their calculations as to what is possible for that person can be inaccurate. It is counterproductive to set standards for achievement that are not, at present, possible, because it is success that encourages; failure is not necessarily a spur to greater effort. Greater effort is not even necessarily the way to greater success. It may be relaxation that is required, or a day off, or praise for the little that has already been accomplished.

In Virgo, the spirit learns to understand the complex makeup of the world we live in and the laws by which the world operates. The necessary coolness of the observation must not be allowed to cool either the heart's understanding of suffering or the value of play that was learned in Leo. With the previous lessons remembered, Virgo is the sign of intelligent, helpful service to humanity on the material plane, the health and well-being of people, and the courage to speak the truth.

*a questioning breeze blows steadily, bridging with a warming breath
the distance between me and you*

Libra ♎
"breeze on a hill"

Now the child is a little older, perhaps at elementary school, making friends, learning how to relate to others, and being very concerned about how other children think. Wearing what is acceptable and being liked are extremely important in this stage of growth.

The emphasis in Libra is again on understanding how things work and achieving perfection, but now it is in the realm of thought and communication with others (air) instead of the material concerns of earth-oriented Virgo. So Libra is concerned with relationships, discovering all the different ways of seeing a situation or person.

Because Libra is about balancing viewpoints, many people mistakenly think that Librans should be making decisions. The way Libra people come to a decision is to gather opinions, facts, attitudes, possibilities, and probabilities and let all this add together in their mind. Eventually, when they can feel the wholeness of the situation, the correct decision will become obvious to them and they will act in accordance with the forces of the moment and create the most appropriate change.

The difficulties of indecision and hesitation arise when a decision is called for too quickly by someone who operates differently and doesn't understand the Libran process. People often make the mistake of thinking that, because Librans *seem* so indecisive, they don't know their own minds, but, in fact, they are very clear once the decision is made.

Another reason for the difficulty experienced by the Libran character is the belief that balance in relationships means being permanently pleasant. Balance consists of honesty and sweetness, night and day, dark and light, breathing in and breathing out, as long as we are alive on Earth. To have only day, or nothing but sweetness, is not a state that applies to earthly life. It denies the possibility of growth.

We grow through relationships, which help us see our inappropriate habitual reactions and behavior and then learn to shed them. Growth requires that our out-of-date skins be shed, and it would be inhuman not to hurt from time to time. So instead of regarding conflict and pain as failure, Librans need to realize that these are part of the process, and, as long as they also help the other person to recover with love, all is well.

A common vision we have of Libra people is, in discussion, hearing them present the opposite point of view to the one just expressed. This can lead to Librans being called argumentative, but it stems from their desire to have all views voiced. This will happen especially when they hear one person being overpraised or run down. They need courage to stand apart from others in the group in order to ensure a fair trial. The worst error, in Libran terms, is to have an opinion that is ill informed—better to have no opinion at all.

In Libra, the spirit learns to balance dark with light, male with female, sensitivity with firmness, diplomacy with honesty, and justice with mercy. It learns to balance its personal needs with the good of all.

deep as the mountains are high, dark still surface, where a summit stream flows in, the water clears and overflows to feed the valley

---

Scorpio ♏

"mountain lake"

The feeling of coming out of Libra into Scorpio is like the onset of adolescence, a plunging into the world of emotions. As puberty strikes, and male and female polarize energetically, the turbulent world of emotion is explored consciously for the first time, often through relationships where sexuality is veiled only loosely, if at all.

At last, the feelings are fully admitted, where in Libra they were subdued for the sake of apparent peace. In Cancer, the first water sign, the emotions were stirred by the need for mother, comfort, and nourishment. In Scorpio, the need is for depth and emotional sharing in relationships. Feelings are so intense that the person can be very vulnerable to hurt. It is as though the Scorpio in us is where our capacity to experience emotions is being enlarged, like a container being ground out. The grinding is the painful part; the result of the grinding is the ability to contain a vast amount of emotion without spilling it all over the place, as the other signs do.

Imagine standing in the country watching the most glorious sunset of your life. A Scorpio person will be able to hold such an intense amount of joy that the concentration can bring union with the Source. The other signs in the same situation will comment, cry, laugh, make a joke, suddenly remember what they meant to do this morning—anything rather than stay with the experience to completion.

What is more commonly noticed about Scorpio people is that they hide their emotions behind their own particular smokescreen. Some will talk a lot about all sorts of things, but not themselves. Some are silent as they observe others. Some are very caring of others, but keep their own troubles quiet. Some keep the spotlight off themselves by stirring up the emotions of others. This is all because Scorpios are more deeply vulnerable than we realize. Their least helpful form of protection from emotional hurt is cutting off from the area of feelings altogether; they can seem to be totally cold and hard, and they are incapable of being happy in this state.

The safest thing for Scorpio people to do is to be cautious in relationships. As a friendship is tested over time, they then become able to show their feelings in safety. A therapist of some kind may be the very first person a damaged Scorpio chooses to trust. Scorpios may have few friendships, but those few will be deep and lasting. One of the deepest areas of sharing in a relationship is sexual expression. For Scorpio, there needs to be emotional rapport for satisfaction. Sex for its own sake is not sufficient, as it can be for the more earthy appetites of Taurus.

An image that describes the Scorpio character is the mountain lake, which is deep and still. One cannot see what is below the surface, and seemingly harmless remarks thrown in sink without a trace. But when the unsuspecting thrower comes that way again, the hurt that has been caused will come out suddenly in unrecognizable form and hit him hard. This is the source of the revenge for which Scorpio is known.

A lake in the mountains can be stagnant and boggy, but if fed by a stream from above, it will remain sweet and overflow to feed the valley below. If Scorpios remember their spiritual home and draw strength from it, they overflow with understanding and love to support those who suffer.

In Scorpio, the spirit learns to know the emotional depths and accepts them, bringing about an inner transformation that also transforms the quality of life. Its consequent wisdom and understanding of the human condition can be used to assist people who cannot handle their own emotions.

bursting brightly here and there from a darkening celebration fire,
illuminating conversation

Sagittarius ↗
"flames"

By now the spirit has traveled through each of the elements twice. It has experienced them and learned to handle them. Is it any wonder that in Sagittarius there is the tendency to express a sense of knowing all there is to know?

Here we find the character of university students, studying what they choose, working in their own time, and sharing endless discussions as to how the world should be run and how well they could run it.

This is the third fire sign, where the energy has to be applied for the advance of humanity. The warmth of fire is expressed in enthusiasm. Sagittarius gets excited about anything that leads to growth and a broader view. All the pieces of information that were gathered in the opposite sign, Gemini, are put together to form a picture of the universe and all it contains, and the missing bits are the catalyst for explorations, both physical and mental.

Sagittarius is the adventurous explorer and philosopher, a student of life. The Sagittarian mind stands on the edge of what is known and leaps intuitively, like the excited centaur, to the next rock, looking back to build a bridge for the concrete mind to follow.

Sagittarians use both abstract thought and creative imagination to assist in discovering the realms of metaphysics. Because of their insatiable desire to learn and their sometimes wicked sense of humor, they make the most interesting and memorable teachers, inspiring their pupils with their joy of discovery.

In their preoccupation with the need to get the whole picture, they can trample over other people's feelings. Their desire to share their bright, optimistic humor can lead to tactless jokes and teasing stories. They may be thoughtless of others' feelings, but there is no intention to hurt. What Sagittarius can bring to the other signs is a lightheartedness, a reminder that play is the natural balance for serious responsibility.

In Sagittarius, the spirit learns the art of seeing pieces of information as parts of the overview of life, and the knack for enthusing others with that vision—passing on the fire of life in a usable form.

*firmly broad-based, complex mass accumulating; weathered ancient pathways
laboring up to a satisfied rest, rewarded with a distant gaze*

Capricorn ♑
"mountain"

As the students in this story leave college and take on the responsibility of looking after themselves, so the spirit moves from Sagittarius into Capricorn, the final earth sign. Here the experience is of the material world with no one else responsible but one's self.

The sense of weight for Capricorn is strongest in childhood. It is not easy to open your eyes to a world where you can immediately see what part you are capable of playing. At first there may be pleasure in the ability to do things well and to take charge, but Capricorn children are easily taken for granted in their home situations, and responsibility is often heaped upon them without consideration for their child needs of play, affection, and caring.

In school, some of these children rise to a position of natural authority without loss of popularity. But others, understanding the reasons for rules and recognizing the difficulties of their class teachers, are often left out of children's games and are considered too serious and goody-goody to be one of the gang. So childhood can be lonely and a lot of hard work.

As they get older, Capricorn people need to realize that they are responsible only for themselves and their actions, and not for the rest of humanity. Indeed, to take responsibility for another can be a way of removing that person's self-respect. It is not easy to feel respect for someone whom you consider incapable of managing his or her own life, even if that person is yourself. Now that the Aquarian Age is beginning, we are all learning about being our own masters and taking charge of our own lives, so the best we can do for others is not to take over, but to encourage them to manage by themselves.

An evolved Capricorn will realize that the material world follows the impulse of energy, and energy follows thought. In this way, things are actually achieved in the world through the purposeful application of thought, and through intention. This requires that the limitations of a situation be understood so that any effort will be applied in a useful manner. The steps that will be required for the flowering of the purpose must be in the correct order and each one accomplished carefully so that the next step will be steady. If all the laws of nature are obeyed and the purpose is appropriate to the time, success will naturally follow. It can seem to us that a Capricorn's success is a gift, or that he or she is a magician of some kind, but this is because we are not aware of the care that was involved. A magician, after all, is one who accomplishes something in a way that others cannot see or understand.

Capricorns like to find some purpose in the world that satisfies their need to be useful members of society, and this is often a family. Then their work feeds and clothes their children, who need to be cared for. They may regard the people who work for them as their "family," and a natural and satisfying Capricorn role can be that of "patriarch" in a company. But Capricorns work hard, and they will expect their "family" to take life seriously and work hard as well, so they can be demanding bosses.

In all this work, emotions are not felt to be appropriate. Capricorns are proud of their ability to put emotions to one side and cope without letting the ups and downs of life interfere. The symbol for Capricorn, Capricornus, is goat at the front and fish behind, indicating that the Capricorn character may appear hard and ambitious. The fish's tail, representing their basic wisdom and understanding of life's necessities, is not what they choose to show, perhaps because it is accompanied by vulnerable sensitivity and emotional response.

Capricorns tend to feel responsibility as a weight, like a large cloak, that they put on at birth. Only as they grow older and learn to handle authority do they discover that the cloak remains the same and thus feels lighter and lighter on their shoulders. It's no wonder that Capricorns are said to grow younger instead of older, and that their sense of humor becomes lighthearted in later years.

The mountain goat climbs to survive and be comfortable in the material world. The mountain is the sum of the achievements accrued on the way. At the top of this mountain, the spirit has a wide view and a great deal of experience in that world.

In Capricorn, the spirit learns to become the "Master of Darkness." There is a danger that Capricorn people will forget their connection with light, and with it the purpose that makes their work worthwhile and enjoyable. A moodiness and even depression may grow, and all joy, the hallmark of spirit, may evaporate. The task is to be involved with the material world without identifying with it, and in this way the natural laws can be applied for the service of the whole.

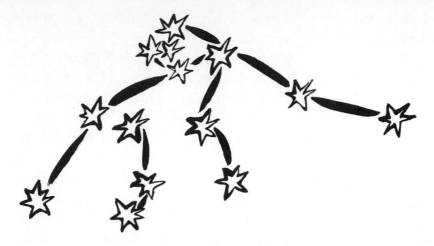

pieces of air caught in permanent relationship, clear, precise,
held in awareness together apart

Aquarius ♒
"bubbles in ice"

The Zodiac spirit's path becomes Aquarius at the top of Capricorn's mountain of achievement. The members of Capricorn's "family" have been supported to the point where they can support themselves, and the responsibilities are all fulfilled. Because of past effort, there is a sense of inner security and freedom.

The broad view of the world and all past experience gives the spirit, in Aquarius, the vision to see how society could be best organized to cater to the interests of all individuals. Everyone must have space to be what they want to be, and all must have a fair hearing. Rules are needed to make sure that all runs smoothly and no one takes advantage of another.

Aquarians, however, often fail to include themselves in this organized, perfect society. They do not feel bound by the rules, however sensible those rules may be. Another mistake they can make is to assume that all other individuals want what they themselves want. Not all people require such space; in fact, some like to be close to each other, to feel the pull of each other's emotions, unlike the self-contained Aquarian.

Perhaps it is the realization that emotional reactions upset the smooth running of society that causes Aquarian people to try to ignore them. Aquarians tend to overlook the fact that everyone has their own reaction patterns built in from their own past experience. It is as though Aquarians have levitated above the sea of emotion and don't dare look down in case they fall in.

It is necessary at some point for Aquarians to explore their own past and discover the emotions that they fear are lurking there in order to understand the behavior of others better. When they understand how others feel, they learn to speak without pouring cold water on new ideas. Their place in society, perhaps as an advisor, becomes clear as they accept the humanness of their own emotional responses.

Here we have the last of the air signs, the ability to think and communicate being put to the use of humanity as a whole. Aquarians are usually right about what they say as long as emotions are included in the picture. Sometimes the expectations that they have of their friends can upset their relationships. While their negative judgment is running, they often demonstrate a complete absence of love, although they will always be willing to mend difficulties with those they consider to be worth the effort.

The idea of love of humanity is very important to Aquarius. Without the expression of love, life can be very lonely for them, but they do find individuals very trying. They need to remember that people all have their own priorities. Maybe a Sagittarian friend forgot to send a birthday card, but this person's love may be demonstrated by a bunch of flowers sent at some other time of the year. We are all different, but from the great height of Aquarius, we all tend to seem the same. Perhaps this is why Aquarians make such an effort to be different from the herd.

In Aquarius, the spirit learns to share its vision of people living in peace worldwide, and to communicate that vision in such a way that it can be manifested by people as they are, with all their emotions catered to.

submerged with no reference point, relationship is fluid—
what you feel I feel, what you are is me

Pisces ✶
"in the sea"

With all other tasks now complete, the spirit moves into Pisces, the last of the water signs, to give what is needed to the sea of humanity. Pisces is like the monarch who has abdicated the throne in favor of the offspring, and goes out among the people incognito. Here there is no identity except for what the moment requires.

Pisces people feel the emotions of the whole human race, particularly those next to them physically or those in mental or psychic contact. They move in a world of emotion where each wave washes over them completely, wiping out what was there before. If a depressed person walks past, Pisces feels depressed. If a friend walks in with a happy smile, Pisces feels happy. They need to be able to distinguish between their own emotions and those of others. With no boundaries, they tend to be sensitive to other people invading their space. They need to become aware that they are similarly trespassing on other people's space.

Pisces often has difficulty discerning which are the right times to tune in usefully. It is a wonderful ability to sense another's true feelings so that you can react in the most helpful way to that person; but the other half of that ability is to be able to let your emotions through and out again, so that your judgment is not affected by them, or even to become aware of your emotions before they reach your physical body so that they don't upset your hormonal system.

Because Pisces people bathe in the emotional atmosphere around them, they often try to improve it by helping or pleasing others. This can lead to them using up their life energy by fulfilling other people's whims and desires. Once they can distinguish between other people's desires and their own growth needs, there is much useful work for them to do, like giving comfort to those who have been seriously hurt, or giving assistance to those who are trying to move forward in their lives.

In Pisces, the spirit learns the ability to remain consciously aware in the present moment, even in the depths of humanity's emotions; aware of the difference between emotions generated from within, and those that are truly another's. Consciousness is needed in every atom of creation for all to be truly a part of that great Oneness, and Pisces is the channel through which the Light of consciousness can flow into creation, so that all can be healed by the truth.

Perhaps it is easier now to understand why the spirit in Aries bursts into a new realization of individuality with such force, with the memory of having been so vastly undefined!

Ways in Which We Are Different

Tropical versus Sidereal Zodiac

When people talk about the Zodiac in magazines, newspapers, and Western astrology books, they are referring to twelve equal divisions of the sky starting at the position of the Sun at the spring equinox, which is called "0° Aries." They are not actually referring to that belt of stars wrapped around the Earth like a massive girdle and divided into twelve or thirteen unequally sized constellations.

In the West we use the Tropical Zodiac, so-called because it has named the Tropics of Cancer and Capricorn. Geographically, the area on the globe known as the *tropics* is defined as the belt around the Earth on either side of the equator, which extends north to the line of latitude called the Tropic of Cancer, where the sun is directly overhead at the summer solstice in June, and south to the Tropic of Capricorn, where the sun is directly overhead at the winter solstice in December.

Hindu astrology, used in India, is based on the Sidereal Zodiac, which is twelve equal signs derived from the distant constellations. It tells the same story as any cycle in twelve parts, the same story as the Tropical Zodiac, but the emphasis of the Sidereal Zodiac is on the relationship of the Earth directly with the cosmos in its entirety, whereas the Tropical Zodiac is concerned with the relationship between life on Earth and the Sun as our life-giving center of the solar system.

Psychologically, perhaps this is an aspect of the difference between the attitudes to life in the East and West, apparent also in the religions. In the East we are seen as beings relating to space, the universe, our goal being to lose our sense of self entirely in the Oneness. In the West we tend to see ourselves as personalities in relationship with God as a single Source of life, like the Sun.

I like to blend the two aims, so we would first endeavor to shift our identity from personality (the Earth and Moon) to personal spiritual source (the Sun), and then recognize the "spark of divinity" within each of us as a bridge to conscious divine Oneness.

Practitioners of Hindu, or Vedic, astrology, with all its precise rules, are often adept at prediction, whereas the Tropical Zodiac is used more as a psychological tool to assist character analysis and personal development. The bias of my interpretation is toward seeing how our experience of life is a reflection of our character so that, through acceptance and love, we may expand beyond personality limitations into spiritual dimensions.

The Tropical, or Western, Zodiac always aligns 0° Aries with the position of the Sun at that equinox, which falls in spring in the Northern Hemisphere. The rest of the Western Zodiac is measured from that point, dividing the circle into twelve signs of 30° each. The spring and autumn equinoxes are those moments in the year when the day and night are of equal length and, as the Earth rolls on its axis, the Sun appears to rise exactly due east.

In the days following the spring equinox, the Sun rises ever further north of east until the time of the summer solstice, when it is at 0° Cancer, at which time it rises at its furthest north, directly over the Tropic of Cancer on the Earth. After the autumn equinox, the Sun rises further south until the time of the the winter solstice, when it is directly over the Tropic of Capricorn.

Due to the wobble of the Earth's axis as it revolves, the spring equinox point of 0° Aries moves slowly backward through the constellations. Every 25,000 years or so, the two Zodiacs, Sidereal and Tropical, are aligned; that is to say, behind the Sun at the spring equinox is the beginning of the Aries constellation, so that 0° Aries will be moving backward into Pisces again.

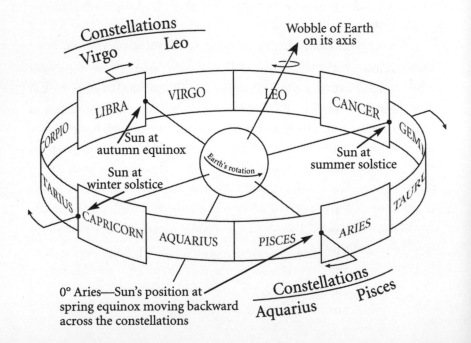

The last time the Zodiacs were aligned was the period of Jesus' life, which was the end of the Age of Aries and the beginning of the Age of Pisces: Jesus, the Lamb of the Aries Ram, was gathering his disciples, "fishers of men," to teach love and service, Pisces attributes.

Having traveled backward through the Pisces constellation, the spring equinox point is now in the area of sky between the constellations of Pisces and Aquarius. The precise point of change between constellations is not agreed upon, so there tends to be dispute as to exactly when the Age of Aquarius starts.

This "new age" will be concerned with using the fruit of Pisces to bring about a perfect Aquarian condition. Perhaps the ideal has been to let go of our personalities and blend with the boundless love of Pisces through service to each other, and now, in Aquarius, we are to discover individually the truth of our spiritual identity. As spirit is without boundary, spiritually all is one, and maybe in Aquarius "I" can become consciously one with life's unity while still occupying an individual body on Earth. Anyway, we have two thousand-odd years to get the message!

All this makes for a fascinating study, but it is not necessary to know it in order to practice astrological chart reading, so we will continue to explore the Tropical Zodiac signs.

Each Sign Has Its Difficulties

We all know people who show us the negative side of their Sun sign. Aries attacks, Taurus is lazy, Virgo is critical, Scorpio is vindictive . . . every sign has its negative side. The following are little suggestions as to what is going on inside people when they display such negative behavior. If we can understand how it feels inside, we will be able to choose a more helpful response.

♈ *Aries* people are learning how to use energy, but they often get it wrong. They are glad when people stand up to them, because they don't intend to hurt or destroy. They need to be encouraged, or they can become unsure and depressed. They begin new things, or revive things that were thought to be over, and they feel the need to keep moving on to the next new thing.

♉ *Taurus* people, at heart, are silent, preferring to commune with Nature. Being so in touch with earth energy, they can heal others with it. They can seem slow or lazy, but they need time to feel secure before they can speak or act. They tend to use no more energy than is required to achieve something, and they appreciate the value of leisure.

♊ *Gemini* people have difficulty linking the two halves of the brain. When in the left-brain mode (rational), they think and talk well. When in the right-brain mode (intuitive), they are silent, not knowing how to communicate. They need to accept and express the imaginative, creative side.

♋ *Cancer* people, by nature, feel emotions like waves on the sea—up and down and up again. They need to be given time to come back up. Cancer people are part-parent, part-child, and need to learn to mother their own inner neediness; otherwise, they will get someone else to play one of these parts, and will feel possessive of that person.

♌ *Leo* people present themselves as being much larger than they feel inside. It is easy to crush them with coolness. It takes much courage and energy to radiate so much, and they need lots of love and smiles from others to keep it going. They need to listen as well as radiate, and it is not easy for them to do both at the same time. If appreciated, they will do anything for you.

♍ *Virgo* people criticize themselves more than anyone else, feeling that anything short of perfection is not good enough. They give themselves a very hard time. They often point out only the faults, forgetting to voice their more appreciative thoughts. They thrive on being recognized as helpful and will assist you if you tell them how their talents can be useful.

♎︎ *Libra* people are afraid to upset the balance. When they have all the facts about a situation, they will recognize the best course of action, but not before. The only decisions they can make quickly are those that they know don't really matter, but deciding whether a decision is in that class or not may take some time. They lift what others cast down.

♏︎ *Scorpio* people are emotionally vulnerable at a deeper level than the other signs. They use many methods of protection: silence, directing attention at other people, or being prickly to keep others at bay. As they explore and accept their own emotions, they become able to understand and support others through the worst disasters.

♐︎ *Sagittarius* people may not be able to prove what they know, or say how they know it. Their imagination takes them beyond the rational, and their teaching creates a linking bridge. Their enthusiasm is intended to inspire others to make their own efforts, not to lead them. Their natural good humor can produce jokes that offend others unintentionally.

♑︎ *Capricorn* people carry responsibility like a cloak, which is heavy during childhood, but feels lighter as they get older. Their innate knowledge of the physical makes their achievements seem magical. The pleasing results of their hard work matter more to them than emotional expression, so they often omit to tell people when they are feeling overburdened.

♒︎ *Aquarius* people may seem cool, but they feel they are levitating over a sea of emotion that threatens to engulf them if they look down. Their detachment gives them wonderful vision, but it will exclude the feeling aspect of humanity unless they have looked into their own sea. Their strong attachment to principles can lead them to be hurt by others with different priorities.

♓ *Pisces* people have no boundaries, which is difficult in the material world. They need to learn to create personal boundaries in order to know what they are feeling. When centered in their hearts, they can identify with spirit itself, which knows no boundaries.

EXERCISES

1. Check inside yourself to see how you feel when you express the negative side of your own Sun sign.

2. Ask your friends how they are feeling when they act negatively.

Negative Opposites to Sun Signs

It is interesting to look at the people you know in terms of their Sun signs. The Sun represents the quality of a person's spiritual radiance, if they give their spirit the opportunity to radiate by expressing the sign.

When a person's spirit is being expressed, they will show strong characteristics of their Sun sign: positive when feeling good, and negative when having difficulties. Positive or negative, the whole personality is holding together, and their light is shining even though it may feel uncomfortable to others. You would say of such people that they are reasonably well integrated, and there will be a light in their eyes.

If this is not the case, the personality will be scattered and the person will feel every obstacle as a great hurdle to be overcome, instead of being just the next thing to deal with. There are many ways of being less than our best, and they are all part of being human. However, when people start to behave like the negative of the sign *opposite* their Sun sign, it shows that they are having difficulty being themselves, operating from the heart. This opposite sign will be behind the Earth and is sometimes called the Earth sign. It indicates the personality without its spirit, so it is a sign of darkness.

For instance, an Aries person who isn't expressing force, energy, aggressiveness, or impatience, who is not starting new projects with great zeal, will tend to seem wishy-washy and indecisive; i.e., negative Libra. A Pisces person who is not being sensitive, looking after someone else in some way, or expressing emotions or reflecting the emotions of others, will often appear to be a cold perfectionist with a tendency to criticize; i.e., negative Virgo.

People who are expressing their negative-opposite state are very possibly out of touch with their Sun sign, and, if that is so, life will be more difficult for them than is necessary. Great help can be given in a chart reading by showing in a sensitive way how these people can change their behavior or thought processes very slightly, tipping the balance back toward their own sign.

When we are moved to help our friends feel better, we tend to go about it in ways that make *us* feel better, but each Sun sign has its own needs. If you know the Sun signs of your friends, you can, in daily conversation, encourage them to "be themselves" (their sign) more. Such a change will naturally lead to behavior that opens the door to their own spirit, which can then express again through their personality. Their light comes on again and life starts to flow more easily.

The following are some of the negative traits of opposite signs, accompanied by a few possible ways to bring people back to their own Sun sign. Many more ways could be found. It takes not only knowing something of the signs, but also a good knowledge of the individual character to find the right way for each person—the wrong way can just make matters worse!

♈ *Aries,* when afraid to act, or staggering from a perceived attack, can become **negative Libra**—indecisive, worried, inactive, going on about different possibilities without enthusiasm, "Yes, but . . .", etc.

   To bring them back to their Aries heart center, say to them, "Just do what you want to do," "Do it your own way," or, "You can do it!"

♉ *Taurus,* when feeling unsteady, uncertain, or unsafe, or having lost a treasured possession, can become **negative Scorpio**—angry, seething, hurtful statements, blaming, vengeful, etc.

   To bring them back to their Taurus heart center, suggest a walk in the park together, a meal out, a day in the country, or a massage.

♊ *Gemini,* when feeling unable to think or communicate, can become **negative Sagittarius**—head in the clouds, can't be bothered to explain, witty jokes at another's expense, wanting to get away, etc.

   To bring them back to their Gemini heart center, ask them, "What have you heard about (something topical)?" "Read anything interesting lately?" Or, "What's the problem?"

♋ *Cancer,* when feeling unloved, or heavily responsible for their loved ones, can become **negative Capricorn**—getting on with their work huffily, "I've got all this work to do," or "The world's going downhill."

To bring them back to their Cancer heart center, put your arm around their shoulder, ask what has upset them, listen, and don't try to make things right.

♌ *Leo,* when feeling a lack of energy, or when rebuffed or hurt, can become *negative Aquarius*—keeping away from people, won't say how they feel, apathetic, etc.

To bring them back to their Leo heart center, tell them what you like about their warmth, verbally appreciate something about their appearance or their style, smile into their eyes, or help them laugh about something.

♍ *Virgo,* when feeling unable to cope, or when their helpful intentions are misunderstood, can become *negative Pisces*—emotional, unfocused, martyred, weepy, feeling useless, etc.

To bring them back to their Virgo heart center, ask them, "What would you advise me to do about (something they are good at)?" "How can I help you?" Or point out how truly helpful they are.

♎ *Libra,* when feeling challenged or criticized, or feeling pressured to make a decision, can become *negative Aries*—aggressive, argumentative, etc.

To bring them back to their Libra heart center, say to them, "Take your time," "What color would best describe how you feel?" "How can these two viewpoints be reconciled?" Or, play music they like.

♏ *Scorpio,* when feeling exposed and vulnerable, or deeply hurt, can become *negative Taurus*—stubbornly silent, obstructive, etc.

To bring them back to their Scorpio heart center, say to them, "It may be hard to put into words, but can you tell me how you are feeling?" Or, if you can accept it, let them express their anger, grief, or pain, or point out the funny side of the situation.

♐ *Sagittarius,* when feeling trapped by responsibility or overburdened with commitments, can become ***negative Gemini***—flippant, superficial, talking without meaning, upset and not talking at all, etc.

To bring them back to their Sagittarius heart center, ask them which of their commitments has the highest priority, and then say, "Is there an adventure in disguise here?" Or suggest an outing or a party.

♑ *Capricorn,* when feeling overburdened with responsibilities and unsupported, can become ***negative Cancer***—moody, possessive, emotional, etc.

To bring them back to their Capricorn heart center, say to them: "I really appreciate all the work you are doing," "It is wonderful how I can rely on you doing what you say you will do," "That was a great achievement (something they worked hard at)," or, "What are you upset about?"

♒ *Aquarius,* when losing their detached point of view about something, can become ***negative Leo***—dogmatic, domineering, not listening, etc.

To bring them back to their Aquarian heart center, ask them: "Why do you think that happened?" "You sound a bit involved, could you say what it is that's getting to you?" Or, ask in a group, "What do you others think about that?"

♓ *Pisces,* when feeling taken for granted or exhausted from caring for others, can become ***negative Virgo***—cold, critical, perfectionistic, etc.

To bring them back to their Pisces heart center, ask them, "Do you ever get the feeling that no one appreciates you?" "It must be really difficult sometimes being as sensitive as you are," or, "What's the worst of the situation?" Encourage them to have a good cry about it to let it out of their system, or ask what boundaries they feel they need.

Important Note

When any person (including yourself) is acting out the negative of their own Sun sign, there is no need to interfere. Most people feel better when others give them their undivided attention, and listen to them without interrupting or trying to solve their problems for them. They do not need help, just the opportunity to express themselves without being judged!

On the other hand, there are often times when people are expressing the positive behavior of the Zodiac sign opposite to their own. Opposite signs, when positively expressed, are complementary to each other, and even need each other for balance within the Zodiac circle.

Aries needs some Libran diplomacy to get away with being themselves.

Taurus needs the Scorpio depth of feeling to be truly secure with people.

Gemini needs the Sagittarian broad focus to bring value into their communicating.

Cancer needs to take Capricorn responsibility for supplying the needs of their inner child.

Leo needs some Aquarian detachment, when faced with their audience, to maintain enough courage to be sincere.

Virgo needs to be in Pisces' selfless service to prevent their critical skills from becoming painful.

Libra needs to be centered in themselves, like Aries, to balance their world without unbalancing themselves.

Scorpio needs their feet on the Taurus bedrock to keep their head above emotional water.

Sagittarius needs to communicate with Gemini versatility to get their brilliant ideas across.

Capricorn needs to acknowledge their feelings, like Cancer, in order to stay connected to those they support.

Aquarius needs to come from the heart with Leo sincerity to have their unpossessive love appreciated and received.

Pisces needs the focus of Virgo to become self-aware in the midst of sensing everyone else.

Perhaps the most important point to make about the Zodiac signs is that all people feel better about themselves when the gifts of their own Sun sign are appreciated by others. If we would appreciate children when they are expressing their Sun sign qualities, they would have a better sense of self-esteem, a better start in life.

EXERCISES

1. Think about times when you act out the negatives of your opposite sign. What would bring you back to your own Sun sign?

2. Notice a friend displaying negative behavior. Is it the negative of their own Sun sign, or of the opposite sign? If it is the opposite, how do you think they could be helped back to their own sign? Does it work? If not, why not? What does work?

✿ ✿ Three ✿ ✿

The Planets

Ways in Which We Are the Same

For speed and simplicity we usually refer to the Sun, Moon, and planets as "the planets." We will focus on the planets in different ways to encourage all aspects of the mind to be involved, and also to assist the memory.

The "Seven Sacred Planets" as Chakras

Spirit is all there is. It manifests as the essence of life and, as vibration, could be described as Light. Mentally it is pure consciousness; it feels to us like love, the force of attraction that holds all forms; it appears to us as physical experience. So we say that the entire universe is illuminated by the Light. It is so intense that, for most of us, an awareness of it in our daily lives just as it is would leave us unable to function as a personality unless we were well prepared.

As we generally identify ourselves with our separate personality, we tend to fear personal annihilation and protect ourselves from this Light. Reflecting that protection, the Earth's atmosphere slows down the vibration of life energy for us, and splits it into a spectrum of "colors," each color having a different function.

We can then experience the Light like a rainbow flowing through our bodies, expressing every level of existence possible at the same time. In each area of the body, the whirling vortex of energy has manifested a bunch of nerve tissue, a nerve plexus, to channel one of the functions necessary to the process of living. These vortices, or energy centers, are sometimes called *chakras*, meaning "wheels." So the energy flowing through each chakra expresses every level of existence relevant to the function of that area of the body, from physical, to emotional, mental, and spiritual, to the reality of Oneness, the Source of life. These functions of energy are reflected in many other ways throughout our bodies, our lives, our world, and every experience of which we are capable.

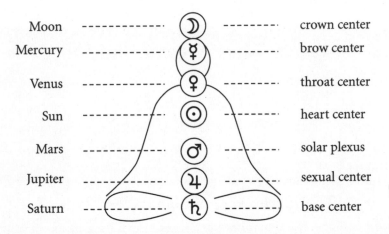

Moon	crown center
Mercury	brow center
Venus	throat center
Sun	heart center
Mars	solar plexus
Jupiter	sexual center
Saturn	base center

The planets surrounding Earth also represent the different functions of life on all levels, in the same way as do the chakras. Traditionally, the seven planets chosen to match the seven chakras involved in alchemical spiritual training are the Sun, the Moon, and those planets that could be seen before telescopes were invented: Mercury, Venus, Mars, Jupiter, and Saturn look just like twinkling stars, but over weeks they can be seen to "wander" through the fixed star patterns.

There are different systems for locating the planets in the body, and systems of meaning for the chakras, and there are different systems of arrangement of chakras in the body. What is important is to select the system you will use like a grid, through which to look at experience. Never be seduced into thinking one system is "the way things truly are" and another "wrong." One learns with practice to "read" experience through one's chosen grid. Each person's experience is what it is for them; different grids just express it differently, or show a different perspective. In this system the seven planetary energies can be said to correspond with seven of the major chakras in the following way (the colors that indicate health in that area are in parentheses):

Crown center—**Moon** ☽ *(amethyst)*—Energy of universal spirit for responding, and playing with creation.

Brow center—**Mercury** ☿ *(indigo)*—Mental energy for vision and communication.

Throat center—**Venus** ♀ *(sky blue)*—Attracting energy for balancing and relating.

Heart center—**Sun** ☉ *(green)*—Consciousness of essential self for understanding and love.

Solar plexus—**Mars** ♂ *(yellow)*—Emotional energy for effective action and control.

Sexual center—**Jupiter** ♃ *(orange)*—Expansive energy for growth and compassion.

Base center—**Saturn** ♄ *(red)*—Consolidating energy for stability and perseverance.

All creation is only possible if there is "separation from the Source." If there is no separation from Source—if everything *is* Source—then the concepts of "creation" and "time" have no real meaning. So let us play with them, and imagine the moment of creation as a process in time. That process reflected in the head and spine of our body might appear as a ripple of movement from Oneness at the crown through many levels of creation to the physical world at the base. If the spine is aligned when the Light of the Source is received by the Moon at the crown center, it strikes the base so that Saturn, as Lucifer, the Light Bringer, is able to shed that light on our path through physical life, teaching us through experience.

Balancing the Chakras

If each of the seven chakras from the base up, or the crown down, is one of the seven colors of the rainbow, balancing and combining them would give us white light. When our balanced system can produce white light, we are tuned to the universal Light of pure spirit, Unity, Oneness.

EXERCISE
A meditation to balance the chakra energies.

Having organized a space for yourself to be on your own, sit quietly with your back comfortably straight and imagine the seven centers as described, as globes on your spine, inside your body, starting with the base for good stability during the exercise. As you focus on each one, imagine it to be the relevant color of the rainbow. When all seven are alight, check over and over them until all centers are radiating their color with the same intensity of light. If this is difficult, try putting an image of your spine and centers out in front of you and balance the colors there. It will be just as effective. Let spiritual Light enter your crown center. Be sure you are safely in your body at the end.

Planets as Human Characteristics

Usually you will find the planets listed with the Sun and Moon first, as the two lights of our life, by day and by night. The others are listed afterward in order of their normal distance from, and speed of rotation around, the Sun.

The following descriptions are in that order, written in the first person as if describing the experience of the reader's spirit. Listening with your imagination as well as your intellect will key your mind into the greater meaning of each planet and each corresponding principle of life.

"Before starting the journey into material life, there is a state of Oneness, which is what I am eternally. Nothing has ever happened, nor ever will, to affect my true state, because in eternity there is no time. Then, by my choice to incarnate, I set in motion the effects of separation, which include time, development, growth, process, path, and so on.

"From the moment of conception, I am growing, reflected by the spiralling dance of the Earth, planets, and the whole cosmos. I transform as a fetus through every stage of evolution of life during my nine months in the womb. At birth, I stop growing in this way, I take my stand, choose my personality for this life, and the reflected picture is shown in my birth chart."

The Sun ☉ (heart center)—Our essential character.

"I choose a Sun sign for the heart where my spirit will come through into Earth experience. Here is where I will be aware of my Higher Self, or spirit, when I am not too caught up in identifying with my personality. At first it is clear and uncluttered. When I am open and honest, it is radiant with understanding and love."

The relationship of the Sun to the rest of the birth chart shows what experiences tend to cover our heart with pain and what can help keep it clear. We will cover this in more detail later in this chapter.

The Moon ☽ (crown center)—Our personal unconscious.

"The Earthly experience begins with mother, who is necessary to me, who is all the world to me, reflected by the Moon sign, the light in the darkness of night, the dual and changeable nature of Earthly life being the dark as opposed to the daylight of spiritual unity.

"The Moon sign is the baby and child that I act out, fettered by all my expectations from so much projected experience in past lives. Out of them, I develop survival aids before I am old enough to think consciously, so my reactions to mother, as well as mother's own feelings and thoughts, are a large part of these unconscious assumptions and behavior.

"I need to be in touch with the spirit love-light in order to shine, and at first I am in touch with it (or not) through my mother. Yet, as I grow I tend to continue looking for it outside me in the earthly world—from my mother to any other context in which I find myself.

"Instead of remembering my contact with the light of the universe via the crown chakra, I stack my unconscious here, with all my forgotten experiences, habit patterns, and prejudices blocking the light. As I become self-aware by shining the light of consciousness into the un-known areas of myself, I shift these personal blockages at the crown chakra and it becomes a clear opening, receptive to the spiritual light of the universe."

The placement of the Moon in the birth chart shows what we expect, and so attract, from our mother and our world.

Mercury ☿ (brow center)—Our mind and its access point between the brain's frontal lobes.

"Through my body, my senses, I learn about my world and then discover that it responds to me. So I begin communication with mother and with all other surroundings. It is from this center that I can see out and communicate with clarity, without moral judgment. However, my habits of thought and my preoccupations, both con-scious and semiconscious, tend to come from one side of my brain or the other and cloud the central view.

"Mercury links the Moon and Venus, as the symbol indicates: the link between our habitual expectations (Moon) and our relationship with the outside (Venus). So it refers to the forming of words to speak or write in order to make that link. When I am aware of the present, it represents clear, conscious vision and intuitive grasp and brings the conscious understanding that I am free to change the way I see things."

Mercury's position in the chart shows both how we give and receive mental communications most naturally, and also what helps us think clearly.

Venus ♀ (throat center)—Our personal love.

"As a baby, I am love, I live on love as a need. I am in relationship with everything I experience as an extension of myself, therefore everything is love—but love of the kind that I am predisposed to think I deserve. This is the attracting energy that draws people to-gether, and if I can accept that people are the way they are, without thinking that I know what that is, the radiation of this center creates harmony and beauty in my social life. When balanced, its expression is through service. Otherwise, I may use it to cover up my negative and acquisitive feelings with false smiles and praise that is out of place. When I want particular reactions from people, the energy stops going out from me. Then I feel needy and become an emotional vacuum, which can only attract other vacuums, with no one fulfilling the needs of anyone else."

Venus and her sign, house, and connections with the other planetary energies all show how this loving functions in our world, how it gets distorted and by what. It also shows the way love needs to be expressed for us to recognize that love is what we are being given.

Mars ♂ (solar plexus)—Our reservoir of emotional energy, which is what gives power to thoughts, and makes an intention effective.

"As a baby, at first I have no sense of being able to do anything specific to survive. Gradually it dawns on me that different actions have different effects. I try to do what will bring what I need, and later, as experience teaches me, to bring what I want (because wants can feel like needs to a child). This is Mars, the motivating force of desire, that acts to be effective, to get what is wanted. It is my motivating force, helping me reach out and control what I see around me.

"It is also here that I am most sensitive to psychic and emotional atmospheres. I need to be careful not to allow myself to be overly affected by how I think others are thinking and feeling, because that keeps me from being aware of my own true state.

"To help and heal another, it is necessary for me to be in contact with, and channel, the energy of Oneness. Channeling that energy as helpfully as possible is done most effectively through the open heart or the clear mind. At the solar plexus, energy is more likely to be personalized with my own drive for survival and will tend to pass those concerns to the recipient of my desire to heal. My Mars center supplies energy for me. When healthy, it will supply the energy I need to accomplish my intentions, deal with circumstances as they happen, and radiate sufficiently to keep me centered."

The chart position of Mars shows the old survival programming from which we operate, which sometimes results in us asserting ourselves in ways that we expect to be effective, even though, in practice, they are not. It also indicates which activities in our lives spark our energy most and where we tend to waste energy, or lose it, unconsciously.

The previous five planets are called the *personal planets*. The next two planets could be called *socializing influences*, because they represent the characteristics that lead us to be concerned about, and involved with, other people, even when we have nothing personal to gain.

Jupiter ♃ (sexual center)—Our growth, through the creative energy of enjoyment, expanding to include everything.

"As the baby that I am becomes better able to control this bodily equipment, eyes and hands, I expand by stretching out beyond myself and taking in what is new. I discover that there is much that I cannot move directly (that which is not my body), and using the Jupiter function I explore the rest of my world, thereby growing and achieving a broader understanding.

"As an adult, I need to be relaxed at this center, feeling free to enjoy the gifts of the universe without losing myself in indulgence or expecting the rest of society to feed me. From a state of having and deserving abundance, I will feel able to show interest and give care and encouragement generously to those I meet. Through the sexual center I create experiences in the physical world that expand me—including having babies! Using this same energy in higher mental activity, I expand my understanding to include new ideas and concepts. By forgetting myself and the fear that holds me back, I stretch out to take the shape of my potential."

Of the many experiences we have, we will judge some as pleasant and some as not pleasant, and, according to our expectations, which Jupiter's chart placement shows, we will tend to go forward and work with them, or recoil and maybe even expect someone else to make things better for us.

♄ *Saturn* (base center)—Our sense of stability, whether as a separate being or as part of the whole, and the difficulties we experience when we identify with anything other than our Source.

"Some of the experiences I have in early life seem to teach me that things are unchangeable, whatever I might try to do about them. These are Saturn experiences, where I learn about the boundaries that define my world. Any structure by its nature is restricting; edges, boundaries, and definitions are all limits of energy or thought that enable manifestation. Any path has edges, and without a path or guidance, my personality would wander, lost.

"The difficulty I have with limits is my tendency to identify with them as part of how I need to be. I tend not to realize that every situation expresses its own limits, which may not apply to other situations. Recognizing this, I realize that I am free to make my own rules about my life as long as I take complete responsibility for everything I perceive as being around me or happening to me. Until then, I identify as Saturn the people involved in teaching me discipline, and I feel them imposing limits and controlling me.

"Only gradually (if ever) will I learn to take responsibility for, and discipline, myself. As I realize how my experience of circumstances is influenced by what attitude I hold, the fear of arbitrary rebuffs abates, and I become able to learn from my experiences. This knowledge gives me a natural authority in my life. At this center I am careful, in building my foundations in the world, to create maximum stability and safety. This requires steadfast perseverance, intelligent patience, and wise flexibility."

Saturn's relationship with the rest of our birth chart describes how we react to rules and laws, including the people who manage them, or our own self-discipline. Saturn also shows how we tend to behave in response to them as developed through all our past experiences.

We need every one of these seven aspects of energy in life. For instance, on the one hand, the expansive generosity of **Jupiter**, which we love to receive and feel, would deplete our reserves if we paid no attention to our own structural needs, **Saturn**. On the other hand, the steadfast perseverance of Saturn can be without value if it is not guided by a vision of possibilities that Jupiter gives.

Again, **Venus** is the personal love principle, creating harmony between people and in society; yet without the energy of **Mars**, nothing would get done and society would collapse. Considered from the other direction, it would be all very well achieving whatever you set out to achieve with Mars, but without Venus to mediate, there may be no one around when you need them.

Also, **Mercury** represents our ability to think and analyze, yet there is a ceiling to our understanding unless we are open to the rest of existence through the **Moon**. However, spiritual connection through the Moon center may be wonderful, but, to translate it into everyday wisdom, we need the function of Mercury.

These six energies might seem to cover the entire human experience, but our personality struggles to survive the requirements of every day when it is without the **Sun**, the heart center, radiating the light and life of who we are into all that we do.

EXERCISE

A meditation to set the purposes for each of the chakra energies.

Sit comfortably in a space where you know you will not be disturbed for a while. How you begin is up to you—do whatever you find brings you to a state of physical relaxation and bright awareness. Here is one way to do this: With your back straight but not under strain, let the muscles relax on the out-breath in a wave from the head and neck, through shoulders down to your feet. As you breathe in, allow Earth energy to rise from your feet to the base of your spine, and, in a wave upward, allow each bone in your back to lift upward, balancing your head lightly on the top. Breathe for a while, relaxing and lifting.

When you feel ready, focus on the base chakra and be aware of the Saturn sense of stability, reliability, and inner strength dissolving all fear.

Lifting the energy of your awareness to the sexual center, feel Jupiter released from fear, and enjoy the expansion of creative possibilities. Rather than let the energy sink down, hold it as compassion for humanity and then draw it up with your awareness into the large solar plexus center.

Here feel Mars filling the reservoir, ready for appropriate action to be directed from higher up. As the energy builds, lift it to the heart center.

There it lights the flame in the center of the Sun, which bursts into a glorious, golden radiance. Bask in the light from the heart until you feel your whole body and space glowing, know that your true self is in residence.

Then, with your awareness, follow that light up to your throat center, where Venus may want to sound a note, hum, or tell you some words that you need to express later, perhaps to someone else. Feel the Venus quality of gentleness and beauty smoothing the energy into a fine upward stream to the center of your head.

Now let Mercury pull it forward into the middle of your forehead, the brow center, and in the flame that burns there feel yourself waiting, poised, looking and listening with clarity.

While you remain with Mercury in the brow, feel a stream of energy from the center of your head move upward to the crown center, and there relax and allow the Moon to open into fullness. With silver light glowing in the universe and showering over you, awake to contact with All That Is.

When you come back down, gently close each center of awareness to a point. Imagine your personal space the size you want it to be and secure before you get up, and remember to be in touch with our constant support system of Mother Earth and Spirit.

This meditation can be combined with the previous one in which you balanced the chakras.

The Outer Planets

The rest of the planets beyond Saturn, sometimes referred to as *transpersonals* or *trans-Saturnians*, are considered to be life principles and, in this system of correspondences, do not relate specifically to centers in the body. They will be described in order of their discovery. I like to relate to them as great guides, each explaining to us their particular life principle and helping us integrate them through our experiences.

Uranus ♅ (discovered in 1781) teaches us about the principle of freedom.

The fact that Uranus is part of the solar system indicates that we need not feel ourselves confined by the Saturn boundaries, the laws as we saw them in childhood. We can break free from past ways, we can stand clear of family programming, we are capable of changing our expectations, and we can observe our emotional habits.

We notice a desire for freedom when we are feeling trapped. We often trap ourselves by taking more responsibility than is useful, or by being "nice" to people in the mistaken belief that it helps them more than speaking our truth would. We have tended to think that we must separate from something or someone in order to be free, but, through the Uranian experience of cutting off, we discover that, however often we free ourselves from the outside world, we still feel the same inside. We are still trapping ourselves through our thoughts about life, and consequently, our behavior.

Gradually we learn that freedom is an inner sense, and we can achieve it without separation from the outside. It is the ability to be involved in situations without identifying ourselves with any single viewpoint or person, emotion, or outcome. If we are swayed by judgment about whether we like something or not, we restrict our freedom of choice. Similarly, if we identify with one thing, we are separate from the rest. Inner freedom enables us to see clearly an entire situation, including ourselves, and in that state we can feel compassion for everybody.

Uranian energy is electrical, the energy most appropriate to our nervous system. When we experience a sudden change in some aspect of our life, Uranus is waking us to new insights or to an exciting vision of how things could be, tempting us out of the ruts we fall into through Saturn activities.

The chart position of Uranus indicates where we tend to want to take our freedom, and therefore where issues around being trapped show up. Its connections to other planets in our chart show how comfortable we are with the principle of separation from people, or whether abandonment is feared.

Neptune ♆ (discovered in 1846) teaches us about the oneness of all life.

We were part of the oneness of all life before we separated into a personality, and, in the longing for that state, we try to merge with others in our world. Neptune dissolves the boundaries between things and people so that we experience merging. Without any boundaries at all, the material world of form disappears and there is only light, spirit, all is One. The process toward this spiritual meditative state is a confusing one, because the boundaries are removed gradually, one by one. Our experience of this process involves gradually realizing that things are not what they seemed before, and that we know more than we did, but that knowledge is not provable. In discovering what is revealed, we realize that we have made mistakes in judgment, and we experience feelings of being let down, deceived, and even betrayed. On one level we intuit the truth about people, but we do not always take notice of that level.

As we get used to each level of subtlety, we experience ourselves as being more psychic, intuitive, or spiritual, depending on which layer has just been removed. It is easy to lose touch with the results and get sidetracked into the easiest way of merging for us, like alcohol or drugs, or even attachment to a particular kind of meditation or a particular guru. When people discover the psychic world, they often get stuck in the glamour of the abilities and fail to push through. Dissolve a few more veils and we can merge with the beauty, love, and joy of spirit itself.

Through our efforts to reunite with Oneness, we eventually realize that we need to dissolve that which we thought we were. We come to see that we never really separated, and that all is still as it was and always will be, one wholeness. We realize that in thinking of ourselves as if we were our personality, we obscure this truth.

Neptune shows us, in its chart placement, the pitfalls of the particular way we tend to merge, and where we can trust our perceptions. It shows us how to merge again with Oneness and know that is our true identity.

Pluto ♀ (discovered in 1930) teaches us about the attitude required to allow transformation of our core identity from personality to spirit. Its discovery indicates that such transformation in the human mind has become possible.

Our first reaction to transformation is to resist it because we interpret it as meaning that we, as personality, must die. The intensity of our fear shows in our efforts to remain in control by dominating or manipulating other people and situations until we realize that it is not possible to change what is outside us. We can, however, change ourselves. Change that is lasting has to be from the roots up, which means that something in us has to die. It is this death that we fear. We know what we would like to have and what we wish to lose, but we cannot be sure ahead of time what is really out-of-date. So we cling to the past, which feels secure even though it restricts our growth, and it is this very clinging that makes Pluto transformations so painful.

When we open our heart to let go of everything, only that which has no life in the present, that which we have outgrown, falls away. Pluto's principle uproots us, shakes off our habits and comfortable yet unhelpful relationships, trims the roots that depend on the past, and replants us in fresh circumstances that will enable us to develop our potential. After the changes are complete, all that is relevant to us is still there and also much more than we ever dreamed was possible. This entire experience can be intense and feels extremely important at the time. All that we have swept under the carpet and pretended that we could hide comes out into the open. Emotions will not be hidden, and words we have held back come out like lava from a volcano. Life is overturned, but as the old behavior patterns are destroyed, we find our true power and can identify more with who we truly are.

Pluto's position in relation to the rest of the charted personality shows where we tend to hold onto control most obsessively, because that is where the transformation could occur. That place is like the hole in the fabric, the present moment of Now, that, if we can get into it totally, reveals eternity. So Pluto's chart position shows where we tend to hold back and therefore feel like victims of another's power.

Chiron ⚷ teaches us that we are not separate from each other, and that the moment we reach beyond our pain to give to another, our wounds begin to heal.

Chiron (pronounced "kyron") has an odd, cometlike orbit. It was discovered in 1977 between the orbits of Saturn (structures) and Uranus (freedom), and this gives us much of its meaning as used in astrology.

We can know Oneness, and yet we continually find ourselves separate in our daily experience. Our spirit knows that, while on Earth, it is our effort to defend our sense of woundedness that separates us from others. The Chiron experience is of being damaged at birth, so it seems the trauma happens then or before. It is an area where we lack confidence or even feel that we are completely useless. At first, those more compassionate children try to help other people in that area of experience, but on some occasion their help will be rejected and the pain of the old wound is then triggered.

It feels as though everyone is conspiring to make us feel bad, and we may lash out at them; what we say out of our pain will be true and aimed straight for the other person's wound, whether we are aware of that or not. We somehow expect to be hurt, so we feel the need to protect ourselves by avoiding those people or situations where hurt occurs. We wall ourselves in with negative statements of what we cannot achieve, what we could not possibly do, and at first it feels safe; if we do not attempt things, then we cannot fail. Gradually we grow inside the self-made boundaries until we feel imprisoned. We are afraid that if we step outside, we will be hurt, but eventually we need to realize that it is not that others hurt us deliberately, it is we who have a pre-disposition to be hurt because we are inwardly attacking ourselves.

Being so sensitive, Chiron people are able to see that everyone has areas like this. We see how people are imprisoned by damaging, negative thoughts about themselves, and we are able to say the very thing that helps find the break in the wall. By focusing on them, we have taken attention away from our own wound; by dealing with the same kind of pain in others, our perspective grows. This wound to the personality cannot be healed from outside, because we are causing it ourselves, but it is very difficult to stop the damage without outside help or a stimulus of some kind.

Chiron is in touch with the truth about people, and instinctively tells that truth. He is the truth-teller whose function is to help us be born into our potential. Wielding the truth, this cosmic midwife sets people free (Uranus) from the prison of their limiting beliefs (Saturn). People may, or may not, appreciate hearing the truth at the time; but consciously saying the right thing at the right moment is healing of the highest order. We need to encourage people who have such accurate sensitivity to tell the truth they know, and they need to learn to do it with love at the right time. Author Frederick Bailes, in his book about positive thinking, *Hidden Power for Human Problems,* refers to the highest form of healing as "waking someone from their (negative) dream."[1]

Chiron's chart position shows where we lack confidence to a debilitating degree and learn that it is our own woundedness that hurts, and not that others hurt us. This position also indicates where we try to do our best to help or heal others, and the form of healing that will flow most naturally for us and from us.

How the Planets Rule the Zodiac Signs

There are similarities between the vibration of a planet and the qualities of the particular Zodiac sign it has been chosen to rule in traditional astrology. The outer expression of a planet is reflected in signs

---

1. Frederick Bailes, *Hidden Power for Human Problems* (1957; reprint, DeVorss: 1994).

that have qualities of air and fire, the lighter elements vibrating faster. Their inner expression is reflected in signs that have qualities of water and earth, the heavier elements.

The Moon and Sun rule Cancer and Leo, respectively. Moving from Cancer to Leo is like crossing the moment between night and day, like dawn. The other five planets of the original seven rule two signs each. Between them, those two express the planet's inner and outer concerns. Saturn, the furthest of these from the Sun, rules the signs of Capricorn and Aquarius, opposite the two "lights," and is therefore said to be the "Master of Darkness," darkness being our experience of the dense Earth.

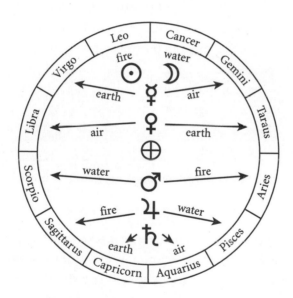

When a planet travels across, or transits, the sign it rules, its energy is increased. When it transits the sign *opposite* the one that it rules, its energy is reduced. Some sign qualities enhance, or "exalt," the energy of a planet, while the opposite signs work against the energy to the planet's "detriment"; thus its positive expression is not as easy. The following section focuses on the essential connections between the planets and their traditional signs of rulership. In the solar system as a whole, the individual planets, the Sun, the Moon, and the Earth each represent a part of that whole.

☉ *The Sun* represents our essential self—spirit-fire. Its purpose is to remind us of the impulse toward creation, the point radiating from the center of the circle, the heart of all our endeavors. It is the outer expression of the light through the Zodiac.

(outer) **rules Leo** (fire), expressing spirit-fire, radiating.

☽ *The Moon* represents our unconscious—the reflector of universal spirit light to those in the "night" of material, Earthly life. Its purpose is to bathe us in that light through experiencing the spectrum of the twelve moods of the Zodiac cycle. If we are working with full and new Moons, the Moon in relationship with the Sun, we will experience one Zodiac sign each calendar month. If we are working with the movement of the Moon itself through the Zodiac, we will experience all twelve signs every twenty-eight days, thirteen times a year. The Moon is the inner expression of the light through the Zodiac, balancing the Sun.

(inner) **rules Cancer** (water), responsive to the moods of Nature, containing.

☿ *Mercury* represents our mind, conscious thought, knowledge, and communication. Its purpose is to carry the communications of the planets to each other and to the Sun, so that they are not divided by their separate existence; and to interpret and express the light of the Sun through the mind.

(outer) **rules Gemini** (air), seeking to know by looking and finding out, communicating discoveries brings understanding.

(inner) **rules Virgo** (earth), seeking to know by experiment, seeks perfection through trying many ways, trying to improve order brings understanding.

♀ *Venus* represents the energy of attraction, relationships, and love. Its purpose is to counter the force that separates forms so that they do not lose touch with each other.

   (outer) **rules Libra** (air), mental harmony, diplomacy, discussion, love of humanity.

   (inner) **rules Taurus** (earth), physical harmony, security, beauty, love of Earth.

⊕ *The Earth* is the nest where new forms are hatched—the womb of physical creation. Its purpose is to feed its children abundantly.

♂ *Mars* represents the energy of will, motive force, the powerhouse. Its purpose is to assert the expression of the solar system (our character), to be effective.

   (outer) **rules Aries** (fire), drive to become separate, activity, the will to express life.

   (inner) **rules Scorpio** (water), the drive to control emotions, reservoir of energy, the will to determine life.

♃ *Jupiter* represents expansion and growth. Its purpose is to discover what is outside the system, so that the assertiveness of Mars will not destroy or damage the unknown.

   (outer) **rules Sagittarius** (fire) through interest, the gift of attention, generosity in enthusiasm, the philosopher.

   (inner) **rules Pisces** (water) through compassion, the gift of the martyr (Jesus was sacrificed at the beginning of the Age of Pisces), generosity in service, the philanthropist.

♄ *Saturn* represents structure, the laws of necessity. Its purpose is to limit the expansion of created forms so that their strength is not outgrown, to check that growth is durable and appropriate.

(outer) **rules Aquarius** (air), in thought, social structure, laws, traditional behavior that secures society.

(inner) **rules Capricorn** (earth), in the physical world, labor, work, a well-built foundation secures a building.

The system of seven planets around the Earth existed in Western thinking for thousands of years. As technology and, consequently, astronomical understanding increased, the outer planets were discovered, each discovery reflecting an aspect of growth in humanity at the time. Each planet was assigned to a Zodiac sign, expanding the meaning of that sign to include humanity's corresponding growth.

⛢ *Uranus,* discovered in 1781, reflected the new social mobility possible at the time of the Industrial Revolution, and also the beginnings of work with electricity. Uranus draws into the **Aquarius** (air) consciousness a freedom of movement, sudden surprising changes, a magical quality.

♆ *Neptune,* discovered in 1846, reflected a resurgence of spiritual activity for the masses, meditation and communication with the nonphysical becoming accessible to the nonreligious. Photography was also in its infancy, the ability to fake or gloss over reality. Neptune draws into the **Pisces** (water) consciousness the psychic and emotional sensitivity, the mystical quality.

♇ *Pluto,* discovered in 1930, reflected the secret development of the atomic bomb. When this finally exploded into public awareness in 1945, it set in motion an overturning of attitudes. This change was based on the realization that humanity had the power to destroy itself and its world, and thus was no longer able to hide in the role of Nature's victim. Pluto draws into the **Scorpio** (water) consciousness the power to use the deepest emotions to rise to the heights of personal development, the transformative quality.

♆ *Chiron,* discovered in 1977, reflects the rise in complementary and natural therapies and personal growth work, as so many people, wounded on many levels, are finding ways to heal and be healed. We realize that surviving through suppression, manipulation, and control creates a prison that restricts our true potential. Through being in touch with, and understanding, the emotions locked into our systems during childhood, and also through being true to our own hearts, we human beings become able to make the step toward more responsible care of ourselves, of each other, and of the Earth.

There is no overall agreement among astrologers as to which sign is ruled by Chiron, but I favor the idea that it might be best ruling **Virgo** (an earth sign), because it draws into the consciousness of that sign the focus on service and the healing power of the truth—the quality of a catalyst.

✣ ✣ ✣ ✣

Why the Planets Were Formed
An Imaginative Story

As part of my inquiry into the meanings within our solar system, I asked inside myself for a new way to express the idea of the planets. I found myself looking inward at what I already knew, but from a different perspective. Allowing a sense of creativity to find new words, this is what came to me:

"In the beginning there was a light space filled with potential." (I saw a circle.)

"The point of an idea arrived from the source of creation (a dot arrived in the circle's center) and began to attract the stuff of manifestation. Where the point had been, there grew a brilliant light, focusing all the light that had been diffuse in space. You call that light the **Sun ☉**.

"The original idea was now separate from the light, and integrated the principle of separation into itself by dividing and dividing into an infinite number of potential forms. Each form also divided into ever-increasing complexity and density, while the principles of their lives were mirrored by the manifestation of the planets."

"Which planet came first?" I asked.

"**Mercury ☿** manifested close to the Sun to express the idea of communication and interpretation of the light. There had been no need for communication before the ideas, because all was One. But as the forms felt themselves separate from each other, there seemed to be a need for a link between them, and Mercury is that link. That is why he is called the Messenger of the Gods.

"**Venus ♀** was the idea that, even though the forms were separate, they would not grow too far apart. Venus is the attracting force of love that prevents the planets from spinning off too far from each other.

"The **Earth ⊕** manifested as the nest where new forms are hatched on this imagined material level—the womb of physical creation. This womb closed in on itself, feeling the need to protect its young, and the Moon manifested to keep contact with the rest of the system. Rolling around its mother, the **Moon ☽** expresses the qualities of each Zodiac sign in turn, a clear channel to and from the cosmos.

"**Mars ♂** is the principle of assertiveness, so that all life on the planetary level shall be able to move about and express itself effectively. Combined with the protective urge, this principle can lead to attack for survival.

"**Jupiter ♃** ensures that life will not express the growth of its forms without knowing how the rest of existence is reacting. Jupiter is the expansion outward to find out about the rest of creation, so that the

Martian expression does not destroy wantonly or unconsciously. Therefore it represents the higher consciousness.

"**Saturn ♄** is the beloved. Cold, fresh, keeping all this planetary growth from its own ignorant or inappropriate advance, Saturn stands guard over the nest, and teaches all beings grown here to be sufficiently in touch with their own truth so as to understand the rest of the cosmos when they actually make the connection.

"**Uranus ♅** is wildness, shocking the nest from outside the confines of Saturn to make sure that the beings don't grow too complacent or too slowly within Saturn's care, for they could remain within the nest for the sake of security or through fear of the unknown. From time to time, Uranus sends out new visions of life's possibilities, using electrical excitement to tempt spirit out of the apparent safety of its many separate identities in form.

"**Neptune ♆** soothes the freed beings, humming in harmony with the cosmos, a dreamy sound that lulls them into a boundless state where communication with the cosmos becomes possible. Neptune is the principle of blending, which culminates in merging with all that is, becoming One in the Great Unity.

"**Pluto ♇** sets the scene for change, and makes the transformation from planetary identity to cosmic vision for any being that appears ready and has agreed with the cosmos to accept spirit in place of form."

"What about **Chiron ⚷**?" I asked. "Was a maverick thrown into this system to stir things up?"

"Yes, Chiron is not the first maverick, and it will not be the last, but it is the relevant one for this time of your growth. Chiron's job is to wake you to your next steps, so that you will see that those steps are for your own healing and not just a whim of the cosmos.

"It is time to grow into another realm of greatness, still tiny in the whole of things, but realizing your many levels of possible awareness and even expanding you backward/forward into the stuff of which you were first formed, the great Unity itself. Chiron is the guide that lifts your feet firmly one at a time and moves them forward in growth.

It is a careful teacher during a painful process, but you will not need it for long.

"This whole pattern of planets is yourself. It is not separate. And each planet, like each chakra, reflects an entire dimension of being to which you become open and conscious if you tune into that planet to contact its principle. Please do tune in. You will be assisting your growth as an individual. You will achieve a greater understanding of yourself and life by expanding your consciousness in this way!"

This is a story.
It shows the unfolding principles
of the life we know.

✡

EXERCISE

Spend a little time sitting quietly with your eyes closed, pondering one of the planets, or the Sun or Moon. Ask inside yourself for a greater understanding of the principle that your chosen planet exemplifies. Relax your body, open your mind, and allow ideas to flow without hindering or checking them.

Afterward, make a note of what happened. Sometimes the full meaning takes awhile to arrive.

Ways in Which We Are Different

In everybody's chart you will find all the same planets and all the same signs; we know that all the principles apply to everyone. The difference between one chart and another is that each planet could be in any one of twelve different Zodiac signs, and these qualify, or color, the energy of that planetary principle. The sign a planet occupies *indicates the style of behavior* that we tend to use when involved in activities requiring that planetary energy or function.

When we meet another person who is using a planetary energy that is in the same sign as in our chart, we see that same style of behavior and we recognize it as natural and feel at home with that person, at least in that part of our own nature. Comparing charts can be fascinating and very useful in relationships. Chart comparison, as a branch of natal astrology, is called *synastry*.

Each planet will also be in one of twelve houses, showing which activities or people in our life trigger the energy flow. In this chapter I shall be looking at only the planets in Zodiac signs, but considering the houses also provides much additional personal information.

One way of looking at the seven chakra-based planets is to think of the Zodiac sign through which the planet is moving as a doorway to that chakra in the body, so each of the chakras would have a Zodiac sign over its opening. It is easiest if the doorway is suitable for the energy that needs to come through. Sometimes, however, the *quality* of the doorway is less conducive to a free flow of energy. In this case, a few adjustments to personal expectations would help get the best results.

For instance, in this system of correspondences, Mars relates to the solar plexus chakra. If Mars was moving through Aries at the time of birth, the function of solar plexus energy will be flowing out through an Aries doorway: drive and assertiveness will be of an Aries style, and the person in action will be fast, direct, and clear.

On the other hand, if Mars was moving through Pisces, the function of solar plexus energy will be flowing out through a Pisces doorway: drive and assertiveness will be of a Piscean style, and the person in action will be gentle, tentative, and easily influenced. The Aries way is more traditionally expected from the solar plexus; in fact, Mars is said to rule Aries. The Pisces way does not make asserting one's self easy unless one is looking at situations and people that require very sensitive handling, whereas the Aries Mars would be likely to upset people by being too brusque.

Mars in Pisces may not assert itself in the direct way we traditionally expect, but it definitely has its virtues in a situation requiring empathy. People who have this placement need to know this in order to feel that their way is acceptable, so they can accept themselves as they are.

The energy flowing freely through each of the chakras creates health in that chakra at all levels of vibration, so that we have access to the physical, vital, and emotional levels, and so on, right through to the Source. When we give ourselves what we need to be healthy and happy, the Zodiac doorways of the chakras will be open, and we will radiate the qualities of the different signs represented. The more healthy and open our system, the better we are able to express spirit on Earth, which has a ripple effect on those around us, and is ultimately what helps other people best.

Planetary Aspects

Every part of a birth chart can be interpreted in a negative way or a positive way, including the relationships between the planets. Some of these relationships, or *aspects*, seem to reflect impossibly difficult and painful experiences, yet what we learn through them can become the source of our greatest strengths and a gift to the rest of the world.

Also, each planetary relationship indicates a talent with which we were born, but most talents have to be developed; very few are completely automatic. So it is that *every* aspect has its virtues, but also its drawbacks when used unconsciously. It is the personality of a person that is bothered by "difficult" aspects, not the spirit.

An *aspect* is the geometrical relationship between any two points in the Zodiac, as a proportion of the 360° of a circle, giving us the major shapes of a hexagon *(sextile)*, a square *(square)*, a triangle *(trine)*, and the line division into duality *(opposition)*. The aspects that are normally taken into account are multiples of 30°, as these have been found to be most indicative of noticeable character traits. Most of these are referred to as *major aspects*, but they include one so-called *minor aspect*, the *quincunx* of 150°.

As the aspects show an energy relationship between two planets, we can start to consider the quality of that energy by putting one end in Aries, the sign of outward energy expression. Then we will be able to derive some of the qualities of the aspect from the signs that hold the other end.

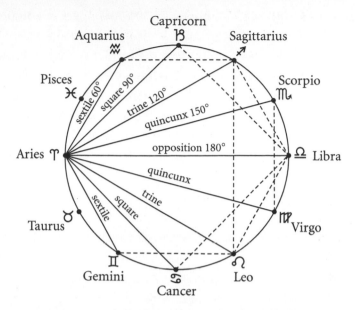

Any major aspect, as listed on the following pages, indicates that the two planets are significantly connected and therefore due to work together as two facets of character that are always triggered into action at the same time. Each planet can be visualized as an independent character on a stage in the "play" of your life by blending the energy of the planet with the quality of the sign it occupies, and imagining a person with that character being concerned with the things of that house. The specific aspect shows whether the two characters find that working together comes easily or whether it requires effort to get the best out of the combination.

The characters may not like each other at first, not understanding what the other is about, but we can imagine them learning to appreciate each other's finer qualities and eventually even working together on the same job. A combination that starts out as a problem often becomes a special power or talent as the person owning the chart gets to know himself and redirects the energy. Sometimes a person is not prepared to put in that effort, so the difficulty can remain for an entire lifetime.

The **major aspects** are multiples of 30°. Astrologers traditionally allow a number of degrees on either side of an exact aspect, and the characteristic will be less pronounced the further the aspect is out of exactness. I always draw lines on a chart between planets in aspect to each other, and I personally use a color code so that I can see at a glance what the relationship between them is like. I give the colors here in brackets. The descriptions of the particular relationships are given next, and they are followed by a list "in brief" for easy reference in the next section.

A **conjunction** ☌ *(circled with yellow)* is two or more planets occupying the same position in the Zodiac and working as one. They cannot work independently of each other, although they may take turns being the more powerful of the group. This tends to manifest in a person as an intense reaction to the area of life shown by the planets' position. It will be more complex and strenuous when the two planets straddle the point between two signs, because then the elements they are functioning through will not be in natural harmony; that is, fire or air with water or earth.

A **sextile** ✶ *(green line)* is 60° between two planets (two signs between them, or one-sixth of the circle) and shows constructive use of the planetary energies in harmony with each other. It tends to manifest in a person as an ability or strength of character that comes naturally. The signs involved tend to be of complementary elements; that is, earth and water, or air and fire, and they lend the support of their different qualities to each other.

A **square** ☐ *(red line)* is 90° between two planets (three signs between them, or one-quarter of the circle). The planetary energies will express themselves very differently due to being in inharmonious elements. Because their styles of expression are so different, they tend not to understand each other, so there is often a conflict between them. It tends to manifest in a person as completely contradictory attitudes or behavior at different times and a blind spot between them so that the person is unaware of the contradiction.

This results in arguments with the outside world, as one energy tends to be projected onto other people or situations while the person expresses the other. At some point there will be an inner flip, and the argument will be the other way around. If and when the person admits that the conflict exists within, the aspect can become an energy source.

Knowledge of the birth chart can be used to facilitate this in two ways: first, by imagining the planets in their signs as characters on a stage and working out in an objective way how they can be brought to an acceptance of each other; and second, by working out, and getting involved in, an activity that would use both energies at the same time.

A **trine** △ *(blue line)* is 120° between two planets (four signs between them, or one-third of the circle). They will usually be in the same element, which allows for such an easy flow between them that they work together without the person even realizing it. This tends to show as an easy talent or skill that the person takes for granted, and he or she may assume that other people have the same ability. The risk is that other people may be seen as stupid or lazy because they do not possess the same skill.

Because the skill tends to be unconscious, depending on which planets are involved, it can operate as a weakness that only becomes a strength as sufficient confidence is acquired to handle it in the world. Empathy for others (Venus trine Neptune) can feel like oversensitivity, and a strong sense of responsibility (Moon trine Saturn) can be a lonely burden when the person feels that he or she must keep shouldering more and more. Once we are conscious of having this special skill, we can take more care to use it wisely when necessary and conserve, rather than waste, our energy.

A **quincunx** ⊼ *(brown line)* is 150° between two planets (five signs between them; two quincunxes plus a sextile create a shape called a *yod*, or "finger of God"). It is referred to as a minor aspect because the characteristics only show when it is fairly exact, say between 148° and 152° apart. The planetary energies will be in inharmonious elements and tend at first to weaken and undermine each other's full functioning.

This can feel like an energy drain due to negative assumptions, like "No one will understand me, so why bother to explain," or "I'll never succeed, so why try!" There is a tendency to expect to gain personal comfort and happiness from outside ourselves, and we consistently undermine our efforts to do that. Not fulfilling our own needs weakens our effectiveness.

Those who have denied their own needs have to break through their guilt feelings to spend time nurturing themselves, rather than just hope others will do it for them. Nurturing ourselves first gives us the health and vitality we need in order to serve others well. Then we discover the joy of service, and all the love and support we craved before comes to us naturally.

It is important not to sacrifice anything of ourselves supposedly for another. Service needs to be a natural giving of our energy from an inner abundance. Any other giving has a sense of need as its source and, consequently, is of no real help to anyone. A quincunx seems to be like a fail-safe mechanism that a spirit includes in its personality when it is determined to remember why it came to Earth. When this personality focuses exclusively on personal comfort, the person is unhappy, but when he turns outward to love and help others—fulfilling the spirit's purpose—the world gives him all he desired in the first place. The special service this person has to give will be shown by the planetary virtues that are quincunx to each other.

An **opposition** ☍ *(mauve line)* is 180° between two planets (six signs between them, or one-half of the circle). These planets work in directions that are opposite, but are also generally in complementary elements. It tends to feel like an inner struggle that we are aware of, like an argument we keep having with ourselves, and it may show in us as uncertainty or vacillation of attitude. The awareness that we have of our difficulty brings a measure of consciousness of self, a valuable quality that is essential for inner growth and development.

I do not use other minor aspects because I find the previous aspects sufficient to do the work for which I am suited, and I like the simplicity. Apart from the *semisextile* (exactly 30°—two planets that do not work together), they are not multiples of 30°, which is the limit I have chosen for my work. They are valid and provide information, but to keep things simple I will not discuss them here.

A List of Aspects in Brief
With Suggestions for Working with Them in a Birth Chart

Conjunction ☌ *(circled with yellow)*—Up to 5° or even 8° apart.

Two or more planets in the same place in the Zodiac that cannot work independently. In a character it will be an intensity in that area that is described by the combination of both planets.

Exercise

In a specific chart, think about how the two principles (planets) involved would blend.

Sextile ✶ *(green line)*—Two signs apart, or 60° apart +/– 5°.

Two planetary principles working constructively together, strengthening the character.

Exercise

In a specific chart, think about how the particular planets would help each other.

Square ◻ *(red line)*—Three signs apart, or 90° apart +/– 8°.

Here two planets challenge each other with conflicting methods or styles, causing an unconscious vacillation of behavior between the two. When working for the same purpose consciously, the planets create a powerful ability.

Exercise

In a specific chart, think about the planets as characters on a stage and how you would get them to work together. What single job would you give them to bring out the best qualities of both?

Trine △ *(blue line)*—Four signs apart, or 120° +/− 8°.

There is an easy flow between these planets, indicating a talent or skill that tends to be taken for granted and is therefore expected in others. The skill is a blend of both planetary energies in the signs and houses they occupy.

EXERCISE

In a specific chart, think about how the skill could be used in a satisfying and valuable way.

Quincunx ⚻ *(brown line)*—Five signs apart, or 150° +/− 2°.

Two planets that tend to undermine and weaken each other. Negative assumptions can act like an energy drain, preventing action. The planets work well together when used for others, and the aspect then shows a special ability.

EXERCISE

In a specific chart, think about what the undermining thoughts or feelings might be, and what special area of service might be indicated by the blending of the qualities of both energies plus the signs and houses occupied.

Opposition ☍ *(mauve line)*—Six signs apart, or 180° +/− 8°.

Two planets that create tension by holding opposing viewpoints simultaneously. The consequent inner argument brings valuable self-awareness.

EXERCISE

In a specific chart, think about how each viewpoint tends to balance the other.

Conjunctions, squares, quincunxes, and oppositions are said to be challenging or conflicting aspects, while sextiles and trines are said to be supporting, or flowing, aspects. It is important to remember, however, that the particular planets involved, and also their sign and house positions, may alter these generalizations.

The Seven "Chakra" Planets in a Birth Chart: Signs and Aspects

Here are some examples of planets in Zodiac signs, in aspect to each other, to show how the astrological information can be used. The exercises listed after each planet can be carried out by anyone, but those of you who have a printout of your birth chart, or even a list of the Zodiac positions of your planets, will be able to apply more of what is given.

☉ *The Sun—Our Essential Character*

Heart center (green)—Consciousness of essential Self, or spirit, for understanding and love.

Your **Sun** sign is the way to "be yourself" so that your heart can be open. We need to express ourselves from that heart sign in order to feel centered. Only in that state can we accept our personality. Without the energy through the heart, the personality cannot understand what is going on in life; it feels as though the light is out, and every problem is like another hurdle in a pointless obstacle race. When the sun is shining and the Sun sign is apparent in our radiation, each new problem is simply what we are doing, and no big deal! Chapter 2 on Zodiac signs speaks of this essential character, explaining how each of the signs behaves the way they do because of how they feel. If we know how they feel, we can understand their behavior, and understanding allows for tolerance.

In some birth charts, the Sun makes no connections with other planets—it is "unaspected." This indicates people who feel themselves to be tucked away inside, not actually making deep contact with other people through operating their personality. This is because their personality, reflected by the planets, is not in contact with their spirit through the heart, rather like the image of a wheel where there are no spokes between the hub and the rim. It can feel a bit lonely, and there is difficulty locating a sense of commitment to most activities, but if these people spend time creating an inner relationship, getting to know themselves inside, they will be creating "spokes" for the wheel. They will find a wealth of strength and joy, like a reservoir, and expressing that to others is something that improves throughout their lifetime.

Any aspects our Sun makes to other planets indicates that those are qualities we are integrating into our central character. Difficult aspects indicate that issues around those planets' signs and houses have to be worked out or cleared in the process.

EXERCISE

When sitting quietly, close your eyes and feel your breathing opening and collapsing your chest. Become aware that your heart is in the middle, being massaged by the breath.

A vision that is wonderful for anyone, but particularly appropriate for the fire signs, Aries, Leo, and Sagittarius, is a closed lotus or water lily–type flower with thousands of petals at your heart center in the middle of your chest cavity. With each breath, allow some of those petals to open. Hidden in the center of the flower is a light, and as the petals gradually open, it can be seen shining through a little brighter. With every breath, more petals open, and the light shines more brightly still. Keep going as long as you wish, there need be no end to the number of petals, and allow the light that shines to permeate your whole being and all the space around you.

Another vision for the breath that is more appropriate for the air signs, Gemini, Libra, and Aquarius, is the image of a bird. You are that bird flying in slow motion. As you breathe in, your wings rise, and as you breathe out, they lower. Fly wherever you wish and for as long as you like.

A peaceful meditation for the water signs, Cancer, Scorpio, and Pisces, is the sea. In this case the breath becomes the waves on the shore, the in-breath as the sea draws back, and the out-breath as the wave lazily breaks on the shore.

For the earth signs, Taurus, Virgo, and Capricorn, it would be more appropriate to feel yourself as a tree, using your breathing to draw life up from the earth, and extend your branches, twigs, and leaves into the cosmos. Later, or concurrently, draw light down from the cosmos into your crown chakra, and send it into the Mother Earth through your roots. Feel for the sensation of the earth's own heartbeat while letting your breathing slow down, and allow a deep sense of Oneness with Nature to develop.

☽ *The Moon—Our Personal Unconscious*

Crown center (amethyst)—Energy of universal spirit for responding and playing with creation.

The Moon is our personal unconscious, which includes our assumptions and expectations about life, our prejudices, instinctive behavior, and the habitual emotional reactions we developed in order to survive as children. Projection onto our world is largely unconscious, so it is the Moon that shows much of what we see coming back to us from our world. Here we are very sensitive and feel the aspects to the Moon acutely, wincing with the difficulties, and relaxing with help and approval. The Moon is where we know what hurts us and what is nurturing to us, and we can help ourselves if we listen to it. We can connect with this side of ourselves through our dreams and our emotional moods.

We express our instinctive reactions most of the time, especially in long-term relationships. It is difficult to remain conscious and aware of our responses at all times, and relationships often fall gradually into a set of habit patterns. Habits are governed by the Moon, so when comparing charts of people living together, it is important that each person be aware of the relationship between their own Moon and the other person's birth chart. If there are appreciative connections, supportive aspects, they will be able to rub along together relatively comfortably, even in unconscious mode. If there are conflicting connections, the habits of one will grate on the other, and they will need to be more aware of how they are behaving.

If both people in such a relationship are working on growth as individuals, they will approach the problem with a desire to become more aware. With the determination to be honest about how they feel, and the acceptance that the partner is a reflection of their own unconscious patterns, the relationship can flourish. Otherwise, they will upset each other unintentionally so often that they may not be able to work through the distress.

Aspects to the Moon indicate planetary energies that are affected by our unconsciousness all the time. When the aspects are conflicting, they are prone to being projected; we tend to blame other people for any difficulties. When flowing aspects link planets to the Moon, the indication is of open acceptance of those principles from birth; the Moon in Cancer will accept them unquestioningly, whereas the Moon in Sagittarius may well question them, but still receives the impressions.

As the Moon is the principle of mothering, all connections to the Moon may show something of how we perceived our mother in childhood. It is important to remember that she will actually have had many more attributes than those perceived, and also that the child's perceptions are set before birth.

Locating painful childhood experiences is a part of many developmental processes because our early treatment, traumas, and circumstances seem to set the pattern for much of our inappropriate adult behavior. But the clue to a healthy energy flow through the crown chakra is the Moon sign at its *happiest*, because happiness prevents any darkness from increasing and also dissolves many of the blockages.

Even in an unhappy childhood there will be experiences that indicate the way in which this child could have been happy, spontaneous, and natural, however brief those moments might have been. When we remember the feeling of those moments, we are better able to let go of the negative emotional reactions that block the crown chakra. Some aspects of our child-state are shown by the Moon sign in our birth chart, such as the kind of thing you need in order to feel secure. The position of the Moon will show many things that went wrong for you as a child, but the sign itself will also indicate what activities would have pleased you.

The trick in adult life is to do the Moon sign activity for the fun of it, not for gain. As children, what we wanted to do was enjoy ourselves, but there are twelve different qualities of activity that may create that enjoyment.

People with the Moon in Aries ☽ ♈ need to regularly let their inner child tell them what it wants to do, and then do just that. They need to let themselves be free to go off ahead of the crowd, and tell themselves often that their way is just fine even if no one else appreciates it. Being their own best friend will improve their self-confidence significantly.

People with the Moon in Taurus ☽ ♉ need to be in nature, perhaps creating a garden for their pleasure, or perhaps just walking in the woods. Imagining that the spirits of trees and flowers are with them will allow their inner child to feel accepted and happy, bringing a sense of security through that silent companionship. Touching trees, petting animals, carving wood, or handling clay without needing to create anything in particular all connect these people to their natural way of anchoring.

The child expressed through the Moon in Gemini ☽ ♊ wants to talk. In an adult world, being part of a group is often more about listening, so these people may be happiest writing down their thoughts and then sharing them later in situations where they feel safe. Although they may be happiest with people, time may also need to be given to the inner child for purely recreational reading, and some form of creative expression will help keep them balanced.

The focus for people with the Moon in Cancer ☽ ♋ could be playing at parenting. As adults, those with a Cancer Moon need to be careful not to become too weighed down by responsibility, and the best activity would be parenting and pampering themselves rather than hoping someone else will do it.

People with the Moon in Leo ☽ ♌ may have enjoyed being a star, dressing up, or performing in front of an approving audience. They may not have had enough approval and love to dare to do these things, but knowing that this field would have pleased them, they can now pursue it as an adult and bring out their inner child with joy through leading children's play, amateur dramatics, or other playful activities.

If the Moon is in Virgo ☽ ♍, the activities would be completely different. These people need to look at organizing something carefully for the fun of it, sorting out a mess, doing a great job of organizing their accounts, making fiddly things as presents, organizing charity work, mending things, or simply enjoying being able to help people.

Children with the Moon in Libra ☽ ♎ tend to feel like one-half of a pair, needing a friend for balance and sharing. These people need to focus on one person at a time, paying loving attention to developing conscious friendships with coworkers, partners, children, or whomever else they feel comfortable with. They may also find a peacefulness playing with color in whatever form appeals to them, with clothes, painting, interior design, or just looking at these things created by others in exhibitions or beautiful homes.

People with the Moon in Scorpio ☽ ♏ experience intense emotions as a natural response to life. The child within needs a careful choice of story, film, or television program—one that always has a happy ending in spite of the tough stuff before it. Drama is wonderful for such children as long as it leaves them up and open, rather than depressed. They may also enjoy creating mandalas: round drawings of color and form that express emotions far better than words do and that lend themselves to interpretation. An activity they might enjoy is scuba diving, investigating in deep water under personal control!

Children with the Moon in Sagittarius ☽ ♐ are so interested in everything that there is hardly time to ask the questions let alone wait for the answers. These people are natural philosophers, always scanning life for meaning and purpose. To play, they need to have times of complete freedom to explore whatever interests them currently, making no demands for follow-up work or explanation. Fireworks, parties, or meaningful conversations with friends, whatever takes their fancy in the moment, will give them a sense that life is worth living. The follow-through and responsibility are for other parts of the personality.

People with the Moon in Capricorn ☽ ♑ enjoy taking responsibility to a degree, but not the kind of overloading by parents or a difficult home situation that may have occurred in childhood. These adults may enjoy voluntary outdoor work, like clearing footpaths or building bridges over streams, as well as dressmaking, or making toys or furniture.

People with the Moon in Aquarius ☽ ♒ are natural observers of life, the odd ones in their childhood friendship group, but still part of the group. These people need to spend time alone just being who they are, enjoying being different from other people's expectations of them. They may enjoy reading science fiction, or even writing it. Every now and then, they might like to do something they have never done before, like hang-gliding, something unusual that gives an extra view on life. For happiness, they need to listen to their own desires without any judgment or personal ridicule.

In Pisces ☽ ♓, the Moon's expectations are of no boundaries anywhere. Fairyland and the psychic world are natural homes to these people. Allowing the child within to believe in these things, they can grow toward spiritual development naturally. These children enjoy fantasy stories, and need to spend time daydreaming to discover what they truly love. Visiting the sea often helps these adults feel like they belong to the world: Its ceaseless movement is an aspect of earthly life with which they can identify, and without it they can lose any sense of belonging on earth. As adults, one of the best activities is learning to be in close touch with the guardian angel they can so easily accept in childhood.

The Moon in our birth chart represents many things, but eliminating whatever habits prevent the inner child from being happy clears away the debris from the crown center, allowing a freer entry for universal love to light our lives.

EXERCISE

Find an activity you enjoy that expresses the sign of the Moon in your chart, and make it a nonpaying hobby. You will discover that the child within is still ready to play, and you will become happier and more creative as a result.

EXERCISE

Using an experience that keeps cropping up as a reflection, see if you can discover in yourself an attitude or feeling of which you were previously unaware.

☿ Mercury—Our Mind

Brow center (indigo)—Mental energy for vision and communication.

Mercury is meant to be an awareness in the spaces between and beyond the many thoughts that cloud our mind, because this is where we get the inspiration to understand the truth of the present moment by being fully present. Mercury is where we can consciously work to free ourselves from our mistaken views, as we learn to control our thinking. In practice, Mercury represents what we are conscious of most of the time, what preoccupies us. These thoughts are generally of the past and the future, which can be affected by us only through our attitude toward them.

If Mercury is in an earth sign, you will notice practical things most. If it is in a water sign, you will be more aware of emotions, yours and other people's; your thinking will be colored by emotional states and issues, so it would be wise not to make decisions while feeling depressed or worried, because they will limit you when you are feeling better. If it is in an air sign, Mercury's natural element of ideas, your mind will be consciously active, mostly with words, ideas, and conversations. If Mercury is in a fire sign, you will be focused on imaginative solutions, visions of possibilities, lateral thinking, and seeing the positive side.

The level of experience on which you naturally focus indicates the kind of problems you have, because it is our thinking that makes something a problem rather than the thing itself. To someone else, our problems may be no problem at all!

People with Mercury in Aries ☿ ♈ think from the center looking out. The mind is quick and directional, and tends to be single-minded. The first thought in a situation is likely to be "What does this have to do with me?" or "What can I do here?" It is not necessarily indicative of a selfish attitude, just an initial personal orientation. A decision might be made to give unstintingly for a particular person or cause, but, when these people are anxious, all their thoughts are likely to be about themselves. Delivered without prior thought, their words will express their truth, however unpalatable it may feel to others. But once they realize they may have hurt someone, they are equally quick to make amends. Their problems tend to be about how to do what they want to do, and they need the freedom to reach their own conclusions.

People with Mercury in Taurus ☿ ♉ have thoughts that move like the leaves of a growing plant, opening systematically, each one beyond the last in sequence. In some people, this process may be slow, but in others it can be so fast they don't quite know how they did it. The process tends to be logical, and new ideas can be received only after their foundation has been understood. The result tends to be remembered processes and well-founded knowledge. When anxious, these people may find their mental processes frozen, which can lead to panic. Breathing deeply and remembering the life of trees restores a sense of the peace of nature, and the problem will be dealt with in bite-sized chunks. Their focus is generally practical, so practical examples and hands-on experience assist their learning enormously. Their problems tend to be practical, and they need a sense of security and time to work things out.

Gemini ☿ ♊, an air sign, is the natural home of Mercury, enabling the fast turns and multiple layers of brilliant thinkers and speakers. So much may be going on in these people's heads that they may forget to focus on listening when in conversation and treat others only as a sounding board for their own ideas. In more conscious individuals, the mind is aware of the importance of language. They know that listening to the style and priorities of others enables their own speech to be better understood. When anxious, they may talk so much that no other thought can get in to calm them, or their minds may whirl among a multitude of thoughts without words. Writing all their thoughts down allows them to see the patterns, restoring a sense of logic that calms their mental activity. The two sides of the brain being balanced this way allows inspiration to flow between the hemispheres of the brain. These people could make problems out of anything, and they need a mentally stimulating environment to keep their thoughts flowing forward.

For people with Mercury in Cancer ☿ ♋, the mind is focused through the flow of cerebrospinal fluid that constantly washes over the brain. This fluid contains the hormonal secretions that coincide with our emotions, so we all experience the effects of its flow on our thinking. People with Mercury in Cancer, however, think positive when happy and negative when down. All their ideas and decisions come out of their emotional mood, originally programmed through the connection with mother in the womb and around birth. They tend to be aware of neediness in others and respond with caring, and although potentially very fearful, they can also be very brave when protecting those they perceive as being weaker. Family issues tend to be their major concern, and this is where problems tend to arise. They need to be able to discuss their feelings and to receive comfort from others, but especially from themselves. Crazy humor often bridges the gap of confusion in their vacillation between neediness and nurturing.

Leo is a fire sign with qualities of the Sun, so people with Mercury in Leo ☿ ♌ have a naturally sunny style of expression. Because of the tendency to be inflexible, they may not recover easily from heavy put-downs and can develop a degree of caution behind the smile. Once they have adopted an attitude that deals with the situation, they become bright and positive once again. Speaking from the heart as they do requires commitment and courage, and the result can feel dominating to others. It is not necessary to counter them powerfully, because, once their attention is gained, they are happy to listen to any input kindly presented. Their humor and sincerity lighten any conversation. Their problems are likely to be around self-esteem and presentation, and they need to appreciate the value of their own Sun sign, which is at the heart of their thinking.

People with Mercury in Virgo ☿ ♍ analyze, categorize, think precisely, and correct others automatically. These people are anxious about making mistakes, so they tend to keep most of their thoughts to themselves. They fear from others the criticism they give themselves, but other people are more likely to feel surprised, shocked, or even hurt, depending on what was said and the manner in which it was said. In an effort to be accurate, these people can sound cold and clinical, although that may not be how they are feeling at all. Their problems tend to be around organization, fitting in all the things that need to be done in their particular area of expertise, and this can create a sense of pressure backed by anxiety. They need to prioritize their activities according to their true needs and desires in life, so that they can give to each moment what is appropriate. This is the most natural and satisfying form of service.

People with Mercury in Libra ☿ ♎ focus on relationships. They are always trying to keep the peace and find the harmonious thing to say, or at least a pleasant way of saying it. These people tend to have at least one relationship that they feel is in difficulty, and that will be their preoccupying thought. A Libran way of getting to the central point of balance would be to step back and contemplate the relationship from the point of view of a benevolent judge, listening to all sides and allowing the correct path to become clear.

People who have Mercury in Scorpio ☿ ♏ think from an emotional perspective. Instead of the unconsciously vacillating moods of the previous water sign, Cancer, there is more likely to be an underlying brooding over something particular—an event, a hurtful comment, an injustice to themselves or someone else. Theirs is thought that creates material results, because the emotional desire is held in a steady focus until the desired end is achieved. Their intensity leads to depth of perception, but can repel or frighten off those who take life more lightly. Any problem they have is likely to be emotional and tenacious, and they need to find out how they may be contributing to it, so that the situation can be unstuck.

People with Mercury in Sagittarius ☿ ♐ have minds that are difficult for others to pin down long enough to explain themselves. They have wide-ranging interests, and are always looking for connections, meaning, and purpose. When tracked down, these people are likely to verbally bounce out of range with a joke, wit, or satire. When their interest is caught, they will study voraciously and share what they have learned with infectious enthusiasm and humor. They have broad minds, limited only by a sense of superiority or strongly held beliefs. These people are likely to leave situations that cause them anxiety, and they may have a problem finding a place to be, mentally or physically. They need to look for the fountain of inspiration within themselves, which allows them to calm down and find rest.

People who have Mercury in Capricorn ☿ ♑ are unlikely to be impressed by any thought that doesn't have a practical application. They focus on making life work, and they are very good at knowing how and when to act. They take on worldly problems, but their real difficulty is knowing which problems are within their true sphere of responsibility. So they tend to become burdened, putting themselves in situations where people lean on them for support. The rest of their character, however, may or may not be able to fulfill what they see as their obligations. When they fall short in their own eyes, they tend to punish themselves with guilt. Relief is found when what they take on matches what they are able to fulfill comfortably. Often their best position is in advising rather than doing, which gives them the satisfaction of encouraging others to become responsible for themselves.

Aquarius is an air sign ☿ ♒, focused in the realm of thought where Mercury is at home. These people have the ability to see the structures of life from a detached perspective, and, consequently, their comments tend to be absolutely correct. Their problem may be finding their place within society without compromising their independence, because although they hate to be classified or pinned down, they do need the intellectual stimulation of other people or social situations. This dilemma can be solved by finding positions where social justice and the well-being of humanity are at stake, where society requires people who are not afraid to stand alone for what they believe is for the good of all.

People with Mercury in Pisces ☿ ♓, having no natural conscious boundaries, will overlap the minds of everyone around. They are constantly aware of how other people are feeling and, in order to feel emotionally good themselves, feel the need to make everyone else feel good, too. So they tend to get involved in sorting out other people's problems and minding other people's business, instead of focusing on, and sorting out, their own problems. A Piscean way of reaching a place of mental clarity would be asking for guidance from the Light in meditation, which would open their consciousness to overlap the wiser aspect of themselves, and the wisdom of our Light companionship, those who assist us from the nonmaterial plane of life.

Supportive, flowing aspects to Mercury indicate aspects of the personality that we can tune into consciously, and that we use when we talk with people. Conflicting aspects show the same potential, but we have to be flexible enough to realize that what is being reflected to us from the world is that conflicting energy. Once the connection has been made, this conscious ability will be powerful.

We need to remember that we are busily creating all our experience; first, by expecting things to be a certain way before they happen, waiting for people to behave the way we expect them to, and so on; and second, we interpret whatever happens in our own special way, depending on what experience we have had before. Twelve people, each with Mercury in different signs, will each have their own priorities and assumptions due to their style of thinking, and added to that are the different life experiences. Every person tends to think that other people's priorities and assumptions are the same as their own. So a person's reactions to what you say to them may well be unrelated to what you intended. They are not being obtuse, and they are not necessarily deliberately attacking you, or misunderstanding you on a personal level. They are probably just reacting to what they would have meant if they had said what you said. People's reactions tell you about them.

Exercise

Try stepping back from your latest problem and look at the judgments you are making about the situation. Imagine how it would look if your Mercury was in a different element from where it is. For instance, the emotional aspect of a situation that is worrying the water Mercury may be slight and passing compared with the physical security that the situation offers earth, or the fun there can be in it for fire. This will help you gain a new perspective on the situation.

Exercise

If you have a specific problem, pause your thoughts for just a moment. Notice what surrounds you, all that your senses can tell you. Relax for a moment, lifting your awareness from stomach, chest, or mouth, wherever you keep it, into the center of your head, projecting forward through that central window just above the eyebrow line.

Then define your problem so that your Higher Self can see it from the personality point of view and, if you find that you really want to solve it, ask for help. At the moment you ask for help, you need to decide to *listen* in silence within yourself for whatever it takes to bring about the solution and, once you know what it's going to take, carry that out. This exercise helps clear away our preoccupations so that we can be more in touch with the present moment.

♀ Venus—Our Personal Love

Throat center (sky blue)—Attracting energy for balancing and relating.

Venus represents the way we recognize and express appreciation and love. It is the way we express ourselves in relationships, what we radiate to people, our tastes, and how our feminine side feels.

The danger at the throat chakra is the vacuum that opens when we long for love that never seems to come. What we are doing is projecting that absence of love into our atmosphere, so we will attract only needy people to ourselves. The solution is to get the energy flowing out from us instead of trying to suck it in, and to do that we need to create the Venus sign energy for ourselves. This will give us the feeling of love inside, and from there the love we give out will reflect love back to us from others. When we love someone or something, we are standing in the flow of love inside ourselves, and, unless we are in that place of love, it is impossible to feel love even when it is being directed at us.

Women may identify themselves with the sign where Venus was placed at their birth, but we all need to be aware of ourselves in relationship with others. Each of the signs of Venus has their own expectation of what love looks like.

People with Venus in Aries ♀ ♈ expect love to be direct and clearly expressed. What others may call quarreling, they regard as honest exchange, seeing it as a measure of relatedness. They may feel unsupported by partners who don't stand up for themselves.

People with Venus in Taurus ♀ ♉ need to appreciate their bodies and demonstrate that appreciation by giving comfort and love through food that is tasty but also healthy, and through exercise out in nature. Dressing in sensual materials, getting a massage, always asking the body what will feel comfortable, any of these things will give the whole person a sense of being loved.

People with Venus in Gemini ♀ ♊, relating through words and communication, need to talk with themselves as well as with other people, an inner conversation that may well result in writing—stories, articles, letters to friends, and so on. In this way they will be able to tap quietly into the imaginative side of the brain, and the whole experience will feel more fulfilling than talking only with others. Fulfilling themselves mentally will give these people a feeling of being loved and appreciated.

In Cancer ♀ ♋, Venus love expresses through all forms of nurturing: feeding loved ones, empathizing, caring, or asking to be cared for. People with Venus in Cancer need to feel that others care about their emotional state—without trying to change it.

People with Venus in Leo ♀ ♌ can be loyal and express their love warmly. To feel loved, they need to be clearly appreciated and praised by a willing audience. Depending on how treasured they were as children, they may need frequent reassurance as to their worth.

People with Venus in Virgo ♀ ♍ care for the well-being of other people, so they express affection in acts of kindness and consideration according to what they feel their loved ones need. They give focused attention to others, and may feel unloved if that attention is not reciprocated, or if their acts of kindness go unappreciated.

People with Venus in Libra ♀ ♎ may feel themselves to be in relationship with everyone, and show it by attractive presentation in clothes, manners, and diplomacy. They recognize love when the people who say they care take time to create pleasant experiences for them.

For people with Venus in Scorpio ♀ ♏, loving relationships are potentially painful experiences, but also rich and deeply important. Honesty and commitment matter more to them than sweetly expressed emotions. It may take time to build their trust, and then it is very important to be worthy of it.

People with Venus in Sagittarius ♀ ♐ have a need for fun in relationships, and their love expresses through an interest in their loved one's thoughts and ideas. If a relationship loses its meaning, their whole life is grayer.

People with Venus in Capricorn ♀ ♑ are committed to making relationships work, and their love waits patiently, ready to move into helpful action when needed. They may not express much emotion, as that would seem to them to be unnecessary, but in difficult times a little appreciation for their efforts goes a long way.

People with Venus in Aquarius ♀ ♒ express their love in bursts. Sometimes quite passionate, they are always afraid of being swamped by emotion, so they seem to pull away rather than give. They need space to be themselves and give space to others so freely that those expecting more possessiveness may experience them as being cold.

People with Venus in Pisces ♀ ♓ are in relationship with the world. Because they tend to overlap others emotionally, they are totally open to receiving, and therefore reflect back any emotion around, so their reactions and behavior may be confusing. This is the one sign where Venus is capable of recognizing love from anyone, regardless of its form or how inexpert or disguised the expression of love may be.

A feeling that often assails the throat area is what we call "a lump in the throat," when we are experiencing an emotion that we feel we cannot let out properly in the situation. As Venus is about love and relatedness, we can help that lump of energy disperse by looking to see how other people are feeling and giving them some loving concern.

Venus represents what we feel comfortable with and what we like to have around us, while Mars represents how we go about getting that. If Mars and Venus are at odds with each other in the birth chart, perhaps by sign or by squaring each other, then we will tend to try to get what we want in ways that push it away.

Venus in Gemini likes to relate through chatting, and a Mars square to it in Virgo is likely to be so concerned with being accurate that the talking becomes stilted and everybody feels inhibited.

Venus in Taurus likes physical comfort and cuddling, while in the same chart Mars in Aquarius gets into intellectual arguments and holds people at arm's length.

One of the most important things we can understand from the placement of Venus in the chart is which of the twelve Zodiac styles of behavior we recognize as loving. Venus in our chart is our manner of relating and expressing appreciation and love to other people, especially our partners. The way other people express love to us will be in the style of their Venus by sign and house.

For instance, Venus in Gemini will express love by having a chat with the loved one. Venus in Taurus will express love by giving a hug or rubbing the shoulder of the loved one. Venus in Virgo will help the loved one sort things out to show their love. Venus in Cancer will make a cup of tea to express their love. As this is the way they express love, it is also the way they recognize love coming to them from us.

If your Venus is in a different sign from that of your partner's Venus, you will probably express your love in different ways. When the signs are in inharmonious elements, it is very likely that you will not recognize the love in what your partner does for you. The result can be that both partners feel that they are giving love and not getting it back. The solution is to find the sign of your partner's Venus and do for them what that Venus would do.

So often we give love in the way we want to receive it. So if you don't know a person's Venus sign, just do for them what you see them do for you or any of the people they love. The Venus sign is just the astrological clue to what the other person sees as love. One word of warning: Don't give love in their style all the time, because they will become dependent on you for that loved feeling and not get around to doing it for themselves.

Exercise
Try to pick out the way your friends express affection, and ask if they feel more loved when others treat them that way. Check it in yourself as well.

Exercise
While relating to family or friends, practice thinking, "Who is this person really?" Then let your impressions open your mind about them.

♂ *Mars—Our Reservoir of Emotional Energy*
Solar plexus (yellow)—Emotional energy for effective action and control.

Mars represents our energy for action, for getting what we want. The sign Mars is in indicates the way we assert ourselves, how we deal with things, how we apply ourselves, and how our masculine side feels. An Aries Mars acts directly, fast, and quite differently from a Pisces Mars, which is sensitive and unsure; and there are another ten different styles.

A man with a Piscean or Cancer Mars will be an emotional, sensitive *man*. However, he may still have an abrupt way of relating if his Venus is in Aries. He may be unable to express the emotion in words if his Mercury is in Aquarius, a sign that prefers not to own up to emotions at all, or if Mercury is square to the Mars from Sagittarius, which veers into looking for positive meaning rather than exploring the painful bits. On the other hand, a woman who has Mars in Pisces, while having an emotional, sensitive energy herself, will tend to be attracted to those qualities in a man.

Venus is the feminine identity and Mars is the masculine identity. When we relate to a person of the opposite sex, we tend to identify with the planet of our own sex and therefore project the other planet onto that person. A woman will tend to identify with her Venus, however self-aware she is, when she is relating to a man. She will then naturally project her Mars onto him, so she will feel more drawn to him if he is like the sign of Mars in her chart. Where he turns out to be different from that Mars, she may well feel that he is letting her down, that he no longer fits her, and the relationship will lose some of its original pull. All this is very unconscious. When she becomes aware of how she normally expresses her own Mars qualities, and chooses to express that energy as well as her feminine Venus energy in the relationship, she will be able to begin to see the man for who he really is, and true relating can begin.

A man, similarly, projects his Venus onto the woman he relates to, and, if he expects her to be the one who makes friends and concerns herself with the loving, while he acts out whatever masculine role his Mars sign and house defines, he is likely to try to control her to behave like the Venus in his chart. When he concerns himself with loving in the relationship, he will be expressing his own Venus and he will begin to be able to see her for who she really is.

Polarizing into Mars or Venus can also happen between people of the same sex, where one of them has Mars stronger in their chart than Venus, or Venus stronger than Mars, and so the person polarizes into that strong planet in all relating situations. The result of any polarization is that we can lose contact with our Sun sign, our central self, and then the personality is in complete control. The other effect of projecting one of our planets is a sense of being only half our personality. Both effects can develop into dependence on the other person, which is unhealthy for both people.

If the projected planet is one that we have difficulty expressing, or represents behavior we reject in ourselves, projecting it onto others means that we will have difficulty with *them*. Accepting that these projected qualities are actually our own not only enables us to see other people more clearly, but also allows us to get along with them better.

Whatever its style, we all need to have the Mars energy flowing if we are to have the energy we need to accomplish our desires. Knowing the Mars sign shows the kind of activity that will get us moving, that will start the engine. So when there is something that needs to be done and the energy is not there, a short time occupied with the activity of Mars' sign (and house) will turn the ignition, and once running we can drive it where we wish. Mars in Gemini, Libra, or Aquarius (air signs) tends to get going after a conversation with someone. Knowing this, when a task is to be done, these people could begin by phoning a friend and talking about it for five minutes, and then use the energy aroused to do the job.

We all need Mars energy in our working life, so it helps to choose a job that includes an aspect of that sign. Energy for a Sagittarius Mars gets a jump-start from planning and considering greater possibilities, so the best kind of work would incorporate travel or stretching ideas beyond normal boundaries. Even though people with Mercury in Gemini may have a preference for communicating, if they have Mars in Taurus they will need some form of physical work as part of their job to trigger the necessary energy.

At the solar plexus, the center represented by Mars, energy can also be lost, seeming to drain away. Some people are particularly prone to that feeling. Those with Mars in a water sign (Cancer or Pisces, particularly), or with connections to Neptune, are likely to find their energy disappearing when worrying or feeling anxious about someone or something. When we allow ourselves to feel negative, we are using up our energy whether we are conscious of it or not, and we can find ourselves feeling exhausted without having done anything that appears to warrant it.

People with Mars in Aquarius, on the other hand, seem to be in command of their emotions, but sometimes that is because they are not looking at them. Above the solar plexus is the diaphragm, and Mars in both Aquarius and Scorpio (fixed signs) can hold the muscles involved quite rigid, thereby preventing the sensation of the emotions from reaching the upper body where they keep their awareness. It is important for us all to know how we are feeling at the Mars center, because that is the truth of our emotional life, and if we don't know what is there, how can we be honest with others?

People with Mars in Aries ♂ ♈ are likely to be impulsive and fast, and need to let their energy run free from time to time. Vigorous exercise helps burn off the heavier emotions and reduces any frustration that naturally builds up in dealing with a slower world. Their movements may seem angry or aggressive to others, but, in fact, they are often just delighting in speed and challenge. Unlike other people, when they blast anger out, it is then completely gone and their natural open friendliness is restored.

People with Mars in Taurus ♂ ♉ operate in a measured way, comfortable with natural growth, not feeling the urge to push. These people need to be in touch with nature in some way, as it will always replenish their energy and revitalize them. Once they have broken through any inertia around physical movement, they have tremendous staying power. They also have natural healing ability, bringing the energy of anyone they touch into a calmer, more natural flow. It can be very comfortable to be near these people in the same way it feels good to stand by a tree.

People with Mars in Gemini ♂ ♊ are motivated by communication through words and movement. Theirs is a light, pleasing expression of Mars energy, but their energy can drain away if they try to continue with one occupation for too long. They are able to do many things at once, and thrive on change in work and play and people. Variety of some kind is necessary to keep their energy flowing, and without it they may be tempted to leave a situation altogether. Chatting with people is energizing for them, as long as they remember to listen as well as talk.

Family concerns motivate people with Mars in Cancer ♂ ♋. They feel their own needs and desires very strongly in the stomach area and can suffer there when they try, and fail, to get what they want from others, rather than care for themselves. Like the tides of the ocean, this energy flows out and then back, so time spent in a personal "nest" will help them feel nurtured, allowing the positive flow to return. When they feel loved, they have an endless reservoir of caring for others.

A Leo Mars ♂ ♌ is a radiant sun, energy to burn. Loving appreciation keeps these people going and may even arouse their natural passion. If they misinterpret genuine encouragement as romantic interest, realizing their mistake can deflate them badly. Positive, cheerful, and easily amused, these people delight in lifting other people's spirits. However, if their positive outlook is crushed, they may drive forward selfishly without consideration for others. This strong sense of themselves in the face of opposition is necessary, or they risk losing their impetus completely. A good laugh will often bring back their warmer virtues.

People with Mars in Virgo ♂ ♍ like to do things carefully. They demonstrate the virtue of balancing altruistic helpfulness with taking care of their own practical needs. When things are not in good order, they may experience discomfort, and their energy flows best when allowed to do one thing at a time really well. They are likely to demand of themselves extremely high-quality work, and any judgment or criticism emphasizes their potential sense of failure. Their energy is encouraged by the sense that what they are doing is of value to others.

Mars in Libra ♂ ♎ is an energy that naturally flows pleasingly. Even in disputes, these people are able to charm the opposition. Their motivation to keep a situation harmonious often causes confusion in their system, as many different courses of action may present themselves at once. This can result in putting off any action until the time for action is past, but if they hold an intention for the best outcome in the circumstances, they will sense when and how to act, and can conserve their energy calmly until then.

In Scorpio ♂ ♏, the Mars energy is intense and penetrating. The people who express their desires this way may find others responding defensively. It is for everyone's benefit that they investigate their own real motives, rather than forcing an issue that they may later regret. Once they have committed their energy to a goal, they will achieve it through a steady determination and will not be dissuaded. Fundamentally, it is the search for the underlying truth that drives these people, and it lays them open to experiencing the darker side of human emotions. Dealing with the deeper aspects of life, they need to be kind to themselves and lighten any negativity they find with understanding.

People with Mars in Sagittarius ♂ ♐ are basically adventurers. Their energy rises to explore the unknown, and when bored they can become listless and even depressed. They easily feel trapped by daily routine, and need to find ways to make their lives interesting. Getting out and about and being part of the larger picture will help keep their energy flowing, but it may go in fits and starts anyway. Rest as well as exercise, and time off for whatever activity appeals to them at the moment, will rekindle their light, enthusiastic bounce that is so infectious and fun for the rest of us.

People with Mars in Capricorn ♂ ♑ use energy to create and build in the material world. These people are naturally competent to handle whatever circumstances arise. They take care to position themselves first so that their effort is immediately effective. What they achieve can look effortless to others, and, taking their own skills for granted, they have a tendency to feel less than tolerant when others mess up. Because they are capable of doing whatever is necessary, they can easily overburden themselves with other people's difficulties. To keep their energy flowing well, they need to recognize what is theirs to do, and limit themselves to that. Overwork is not healthy and ends in breakdown, so rest and change need to be programmed into their schedule.

It is not easy to understand people with Mars in Aquarius ♂ ♒. Running on nervous energy, they can be out of touch with the state of their body. Their motives are for the common good, but they tend to limit their involvement to discussion rather than action. They may give others a sense that they know what is right, and although this may be true, it also may not be true, depending on other factors in their personality. An indication that they need to take a break is when they become angry or heavily judgmental in an open discussion. By taking time to relax by themselves, their nervous system can recover, bringing back their natural quality of calm detachment.

Pisces ♂ ♓, having no boundaries, is a vulnerable sign in which to have Mars in a birth chart. However giving we may be, we each need our own energy to keep our bodies healthy, but these people's energy tends to flow out from themselves unchecked, damaging their self-image and putting their health at risk. These people are in contact with all creation, whether they know it or not. Their open solar plexus constantly receives impressions from their surroundings so that they are not sure where they end and others begin. It is essential that they pay attention to their own needs and take care of those first, so that they are clearer about what actions will really help others. They need not be embarrassed by their emotions, which often express, and defuse, what others have been holding back.

EXERCISE

While being quiet with yourself, put your attention in your solar plexus and ask if there is anything it wishes to say to you. You can use the chart placement of your Mars to give you clues as to the kind of issue that might need to be examined.

EXERCISE

When there is something you want to achieve, check out what in that achievement will inspire the driving motivation of your Mars sign. Then practice deliberately invoking the energy at the Mars center by focusing on that aspect of the task. As the energy awakens, use it to power your original desire into an intention. Emotional energy is one step nearer than thought to the vibration of the material world, and brings ideas further into manifestation.

♃ *Jupiter—Our Growth*

Sexual center (orange)—Expansive energy for growth and compassion.

Jupiter represents our growth as individuals and our expansion in the world. The energy is triggered by pleasure in life. Whether enjoying ourselves physically, emotionally, mentally, or spiritually, we reach out beyond what is necessary, setting in motion the creative flow of giving and receiving.

We reach out on the physical level through bodily contact or sound or movement, and on the emotional level through sympathy and feeling for someone else's experience. On the mental level we extend interest, and on the spiritual level, compassion. Because we are operating without fear at those times, we find ourselves doing things in new ways and finding creative solutions, revealing those potential gifts that others may have suspected in us but that we were afraid to acknowledge.

The Jupiter sign shows the kind of encouragement we need to stretch out and grow, and also the way in which we encourage others. Support, interest, and acceptance need to be received in order to be given out to others, but we allow ourselves to receive them only if we have confidence that we deserve them. Without that sense of deserving, we cannot recognize encouragement when it is given.

For those of us whose old expectations of rejection or criticism created a childhood without acceptance and encouragement, there is a need to develop an acceptance and love of ourselves, to give ourselves permission to be as we are, rather than constantly try to be what we think others want us to be. When we give ourselves permission to enjoy the sign (and house) of Jupiter, one way or another other people will benefit from the flow. Everybody enjoys the energy of Jupiter, the beneficent "father of the gods" who creates a sense of abundant possibilities.

People with Jupiter in Capricorn are expansive in practical ways. They enjoy developing a growing business or making plans to move to a better home. They are generous with advice about practical arrangements, and ready to take responsibility for situations that they create. They are always ready to do what is necessary, with good feeling, so it is a pleasure to work with them.

Jupiter in Aries would seem to be the antithesis of generosity because Aries is traditionally so self-involved, but as children their confidence grows if allowed to be independent when they are ready, allowed to do things their own way, rather than either having to be obedient, or being rejected and having to manage on their own before they are competent. Then, when they are able to enjoy having their own autonomy, they will encourage other people to be themselves and do their own thing; they will inspire the courage to be honest and give of one's self freely by example.

People with Jupiter in Cancer, on the other hand, need mothering care and emotional support. The emotional neediness of these people could easily hold back their growth, and they need to learn to give themselves gentle support and nurturing, so that they have within themselves enough to give from. Their way of encouraging others is to give them the support of caring love and kindness. They enjoy providing a home for those in need, sharing their space, and being solicitous of other people's feelings.

When Jupiter aspects another planet in a birth chart, it always increases whatever energy and activity are represented by that planet in its sign and house. When the aspect is an opposition, Jupiter tends to have overly high expectations of the performance of the other planet.

When the aspect to another planet is a square, the generosity of Jupiter is "over the top," too much of a good thing, reflecting a tendency to overdo the activity represented by the other planet until there is a need to retreat and recover, and the activity stops altogether for a while. This vacillation can be awkward until we learn to moderate the swings, taking care of our needs before becoming exhausted.

Jupiter square Mars shows a tendency to feel overoptimistic about what we can achieve. Not allowing for limitations, effort is put in to master the situation until our energy runs out and we withdraw completely, feeling apathy or illness, or anger at our inability to achieve the desired result. This can clearly be remedied as we learn to pace ourselves. It is very important, wherever Jupiter is in the chart, to be active in that area of life because that is where the enjoyment lies that will unlock our potential.

Jupiter energy is for us to grow, to unfold into all that we can be. There are two pitfalls we need to resist. One is the tendency to give it all to other people hoping for approval, which is depleting. The other is expecting other people to give us all we need as our right or as a continuation of childhood; this completely stunts our growth, blocking the giving-and-receiving pipe. Neither of these mistakes feels pleasant for the person who is acting that way. When we give generously without expecting return, we naturally receive because the pipe is open and flowing. The trick is to find the enjoyment for ourselves, and exploring the house and sign of our Jupiter can give clues as to what activities will supply that enjoyment.

EXERCISE

Find an activity that relates to the style of the sign and house in which Jupiter is placed in your chart; make sure that you allow yourself the enjoyment of exploring that activity. Practice enjoying whatever you do. Look for the enjoyable part of every situation and focus on that, noticing the new ways you find to do things. Notice when fear stops you, and, without being foolhardy, see if you can encourage yourself to follow through.

♄ Saturn—Our Sense of Stability

Base center (red)—Consolidating energy for stability and perseverance.

Saturn represents our balance point, or taproot in the Earth, our foundation. It is also the wisdom gained as we work to take responsibility for all our experiences in life. When we are children, adults have authority over us and discipline us, so we naturally project our Saturn onto them. We project outside ourselves the energy of structuring and limiting, like offering the world the handle of our Saturn with which to control us. Thereafter we are predisposed to react to similar situations and people in the way in which the rest of our birth chart relates to Saturn. Some people never grow past that stage, always blaming other people for what they consider to be wrong with their lives. The original disciplining parent is reflected in the boss, or the government, or an irritating neighbor—anyone but themselves.

Blaming someone else for our troubles, we take on the role of victim, powerless and out of control of our life. When we feel as adults that someone else has authority over us, we either behave like irresponsible children again, or, in the small area where we may have power, we try to control through enforcing rigid, inflexible behavior and rules.

Until we have endeavored to establish some mastery of the Saturn sign through self-discipline, we will feel a sense of insecurity that will limit our ability to be the authority in our own lives. We will fear difficult experiences (victim mode) or feel anxiety about failure (the hard time we give ourselves). We gain the power of true authority only by accepting that everything in our life belongs to us, that it all fits in some way or it would not be there. One way or another, we created it, either by choosing on one level to experience it, or simply through the way we read life with our particular assumptions and expectations.

As a guide, Saturn will not let us step into the power of success unless we are secure in our own self. In practice this shows as the structures, circumstances, and necessities of our life. So the Saturn sign shows our style of inner work, of self-discovery. It shows how we persevere with the systematic uncovering of our unconsciousness, helping clear the crown (Moon) chakra.

As this inner work proceeds, the light of consciousness travels down the spine to awaken the energy lying coiled and waiting at the base chakra. As it rises, that light creates the staff on which we can rely, a vibrant strength of our own, and the inner wisdom that guides us. That sense of inner strength enables us to be responsive to situations; maturity allows for flexibility. We know we will always be able to cope with life because we allow life to teach us how.

Saturn in Gemini is about learning to govern the processes of your mind. If you have Mercury in Pisces, for example, this will not be an easy task, because your natural method of thought is very unfocused and without logic. But whenever there is a self-disciplined effort to think clearly, the logic can be formidable—Saturn drawing the lines of reason inexorably. Saturn in Gemini goes more easily with Mercury in Aquarius, for example, showing a personality whose mind normally thinks in organized patterns.

People with Saturn in Scorpio are being asked to look for their taproot in the deepest emotions. They will have been born knowing, or will have learned in childhood, that it wasn't safe to express that level of feeling. So the tendency will be to keep it all under control, if that is possible. In order to gain a sense of inner security, they will need to learn to be aware of what their emotions really are, and what to do with them, choosing the path of taking responsibility for them rather than blaming someone else. This will give them a stature with others that makes them believable in positions as counselors, psychotherapists, or overseeing people in any capacity.

Saturn in Pisces, the sign of no boundaries, indicates a childhood where discipline was unclear and finding boundaries was a puzzle. In later life there is a tendency to express rules dogmatically and then change them. These are people who will be strengthened by locating a familiar set of spiritual or humanitarian principles by which to live. They may need to shut other people out of their space at times in order to persevere with the necessary work to achieve their goals, and they may be assisted in this by working in a soft, aesthetic, or peaceful environment.

Any personal planet square to Saturn will indicate a part of the personality that tends to be antagonized or hurt by authority, depending on the planet and where it is placed. This will be the area where the person has a difficulty with self-discipline, and yet systematic efforts to be organized will be rewarded with great achievements. As with all square aspects, once the two work together, a new energy is released. For instance, Saturn in Aquarius square Mercury in Scorpio shows an emotional way of looking at life that tends to see authority as cold and hard. However, when these two functions are working together, the personality could be a humanitarian speaker capable of moving the hardest heart.

Aspects from Saturn tend to indicate a sense of anxiety and lack of confidence until these people have become proficient in their field somewhat later in life. This will go along with an easing of manner, because it is the tension of fear that creates the rigid control. Saturn conjunct, sextile, or trine a personal planet is likely to reflect a person who seemed old and wise even in the cradle.

An unaspected Saturn indicates people who can only get things organized on their own. It is very important for these people to know this, because if they try to work like others, they will develop a sense of being totally incapable of organizing anything. Yet when no other part of the personality is being triggered by other people, they will actually be more efficient than most because there are no inner distractions.

Saturn is about taking responsibility for what we experience in our life, recognizing that the way our life seems to be is a result of what we expect. As we accept this, taking care not to identify with what we have created or with the personality that creates it, we will find our true identity rooted in the Oneness of all life.

EXERCISE

Look at your life in terms of the rules you felt you had to obey, the things you thought you had to do or must not do. The element your Saturn is in will give a clue as to the level of life where you felt restricted. Then systematically work out what you gained through being limited in those ways. Accept the way it has been, and then ask yourself if some of those rules could be changed, and what other rules you could replace them with.

The Outer Planets in Aspect to the Seven Inner Planets

The outer planets are easier to understand in a birth chart if we look at them in relationship with the inner seven. It is as though the outer planets teach us their principles through specific chakra connections. If there are no aspects between an outer planet and any of the chakra planets in the birth chart, then that outer planetary principle will not have a high priority in the person's consciousness. The principle will tend to arise as an issue only when that outer planet triggers a chakra planet through its movement, its transit, through the Zodiac. This might be experienced as a surprise inner change or event in life.

The following are some examples of outer planets aspecting chakra planets. When these aspects feel uncomfortable, it indicates that we are having trouble understanding the relevance of the planets' impersonal principles. What is needed is often a different way of looking at what appears to be going on.

⛢ *Uranus* teaches us about the principle of freedom.

In our bodies, Uranus rules the nervous system. When it is in relationship with Mars in a birth chart, it indicates that the energy we use is largely nervous energy. It feels exciting or frightening, depending on our attitude to change.

A square aspect, opposition, or quincunx to Mars from Uranus shows that our nervous system will tend to be depleted by the speedy way we go about life, so that we become very tense and subsequently exhausted. There is a need for us to respect our nervous system as though it were a hothouse plant, give ourselves the relevant food and vitamins, and regularly allowing ourselves times of freedom from inner pressure to relax with a massage, time to read a book, or whatever else works.

Uranus in aspect to Venus refers to feelings of separation in relationships, which usually indicates a sense of either loneliness or aloneness. A trine or sextile shows an easy sense of detachment, which is a helpful quality in jobs like counseling, partly because we feel safer talking to someone who seems to be unaffected by what we are saying, and partly because the people with the aspect will not deplete themselves by worrying about clients in their free time.

A square, opposition, or quincunx from Uranus to Venus indicates that issues of abandonment and loss may be leftover from traumatic experiences early in this life and before, and there could be a fear of separating from a loved one. We could be much supported knowing that on the mental and emotional levels of life, we are always together with those we love. If we have been clinging to a relationship with the unconscious fear that we cannot survive on our own, we may need freedom from it. Only in that space may we discover that we are strong enough to cope with our own suffering personality, which may well dispense with most of the suffering.

In relationship with Mercury, Uranus indicates an electrical quality of mental activity. This produces flashes of inspired vision alternating with blank patches. Uncomfortable aspects indicate difficulty dealing with the blanks, which may ease when we learn to ask questions inwardly and wait for the answers to become clear. The silence of the blanks allows insights to arise.

Whether we feel a need for freedom or a fear of being freed, we need to be aware that both attitudes trap us into particular emotions and choices of behavior. True inner freedom comes through a non-judgmental acceptance of what is there so that we are not pulled by those instinctive emotional reactions.

♆ *Neptune* teaches us about the oneness of all life and the principle of trust that is needed to approach it.

An aspect from Neptune to Mercury, Venus, Mars, the Sun, or the Moon indicates that we have no boundaries between ourselves and others. This means that we easily empathize with and intuit other people's thoughts and emotions, and tend to pick up, without noticing, other people's issues.

The trine indicates that we don't see this as a problem and expect others to be equally sensitive. The square indicates that we find it a problem, feeling ourselves to be overly sensitive and invaded by others. Another difficulty stemming from a lack of boundaries is the tendency to trespass on the space of others, because we feel our space is everywhere.

To merge and become one with life, we need to completely relax, to trust life inwardly. When Neptune is square to a personal planet, it indicates that we tend to misplace that trust by not paying attention to our intuition. We have very high ideals that we try to live up to, and hope that other people will live up to them, too. Trying to live up to high ideals often means not accepting behavior in ourselves or others that we consider to be less than ideal. When we do this, we tend to attract people who mirror to us our own rejected qualities. In presenting a false impression, we are deceived by others in return, or misread them by giving them "the benefit of the doubt." When others act out those rejected qualities, we feel disappointed, let down, and even betrayed.

What is needed here is acceptance of the way we, and other people, actually are, even though we may not know what that is; this is our starting point. Ideals are like stars to a sailor, guiding our choices in the world. If we reject the way things are in favor of the way we would like them to be, we have no starting point and we get lost.

Accepting ourselves the way we are means being totally honest with ourselves and with our world. When we do that, people can't help revealing themselves to us, we get to see who they really are, and we are not surprised by them later on.

When we speak of trusting others, it often means that we expect certain behavior from them, which is unfair. We need to trust ourselves in relationship with life, and trust that we will be able to handle whatever situations arise, no matter whether others fulfill our expectations of them or not. It is the essential self in each person that we can trust as being part of the essence of life.

With Neptune square Mars, we are extremely sensitive to others to our own detriment. As Mars corresponds to the solar plexus, we may suffer from stomach tension as an effort to prevent ourselves from always reacting to other people's emotions. This reservoir of energy can be misdirected because we think we know what others are feeling and why; and with the Neptune square, although we pick up correct information, there is a tendency to misinterpret it according to our fears.

We need to be more aware of our own feelings when we are with other people, to steady ourselves, and when feeling guilty about another person's hurt or anger, to remember that we may well not be the cause. Because personalities, by their nature, are separate, any sense of blending with another personality is an illusion. We may be projecting our identity onto them because they mirror us so well; or we may be overlapping their space so that we feel their feelings and think their thoughts. We must be careful not to lose ourselves in their issues, or clutter their space with our feelings and thoughts.

As the veils between our understanding and the reality of Oneness gradually disappear, we may experience confusion and increased sensitivity in the element and house Neptune occupies in our chart, and through the placement of the chakra planet aspected by Neptune. We may experience psychic phenomena, informative dreams, or increased spiritual awareness, depending on our level of operation. True blending can only be with that which is common to all existence, spirit, or the essence of life itself.

♇ *Pluto* teaches us about the attitude required to allow the transformation of our identity from our separate personality toward universal spirit, as the caterpillar transforms into a butterfly, its identity as a caterpillar dying in the process.

Because it deals with death and transformation, Pluto tends to be feared. Most of us have a desire to control the way things are in order to avoid that death, because, from the personality point of view, the transformation is not understood. Our own particular terrors are shown by Pluto's position in the birth chart, and the planets that it aspects will be the chakras that we try to control. We fear that this death will come from the outside, so maintaining control feels essential to survival; but we are actually projecting our power into our world instead of recognizing it as our own, which is why the world seems so frightening.

We use manipulation, domination, and all kinds of power games to keep death away. Like a lid on a volcano, this is no use, and the longer we hold it down, the bigger the explosion in the end. Pluto's aim is to penetrate us to the roots, bringing into the open all that we have tried to hide away, because with transformation nothing is left untouched. Usually the transformation comes about through a situation that develops or arrives in life that we cannot deal with at our current level of understanding. There is a need for us to accept that, like a growing snake, we, too, will feel more comfortable, more ourselves, when we allow our outgrown skin—attitudes, assumptions, judgments—to fall away.

Pluto trine a planet shows that there is an acceptance of this principle. The transformations are still not easy, but they tend to be understood as they are happening. Pluto squares indicate a harder fight, clinging to the past more desperately. The identity is so fixed in some aspect of the personality that it feels as though we ourselves will not survive if we let it go.

Pluto aspects to Venus are about clinging to relationships obsessively until the other person feels suffocated and leaves, or rejecting relationships so that we do not have to suffer being rejected; any expectations of disaster cause the Venus to create disaster. There is a need here for the feminine aspect of the personality to be given tender loving care, to be appreciated and healed in spite of the negative emotions that it contains. Sometimes this is easier to do by visualizing how Venus as a woman would look in the sign she occupies, and seeing her as a separate character in a life where the triggering trauma took place. Once she is acknowledged, she can tell of her pain, and we can accept and love her.

Any outer experience of rejection is simply a reflection of what we are already doing to ourselves. If we accept ourselves, however unacceptable we fear we may be, we will see that other people are not rejecting us in truth; they, like us, are dealing with their own problems in the only way they know how. Having found and accepted the fearful, possessive, suffering part of ourselves, we can see beyond it, which may largely be the transformation itself.

Pluto requires that we be prepared to let go of past memories and all future plans. We need to develop an attitude of completely open adaptability to the power of the moment, and whatever events and changes it brings. We need to let go of our attachment to every characteristic of the person we have thought ourselves to be. In transforming, we will be different, and there is no way of knowing beforehand how we will be afterward.

♔ *Chiron* teaches us that we are not separate from each other, and that the moment we reach beyond our pain to give to another, we start to heal our wounds.

The planets that Chiron aspects in the chart tend to be facets of character that seem to be damaged at, or before, birth. Squares, oppositions, and quincunxes are likely to be more damaged, but trines and sextiles can also be painfully affected. The wounded feeling can range from a slight lack of confidence around those characteristics, to a fear of expressing them at all, which freezes our energy. Because Chiron is a fairly recent discovery, I am providing notes here on all the possible Zodiac positions, developed by exploring other people's experiences while reading their charts. My motivation to make this inquiry is, not surprisingly, reflected by Chiron having a prime placement in my own birth chart!

For each of the twelve Zodiac placements of Chiron, these are four questions we could ask about the person. The answers to the first of these questions show the wonderful work that people can achieve even though they began this life feeling small and helpless, hiding from the pain that always seemed to be inflicted by an insensitive world. Those gifts arise as each individual recognizes a common humanity with others and, with compassion, speaks out about what they know in spite of possible ridicule or reprisals, or does what is needed even if it goes against tradition.

Through their courage, they bring healing to people and situations, and as they move forward in this way they are, in fact, supported by life. It is this that brings the longed-for healing for these people—an end to the negativity they pour over themselves.

In any individual case, the answers will be more complex than those given here, due to other planetary aspects and the specific houses involved. It should also be remembered, as always, that each person's experience is unique; an astrologer can only point to the kinds of feeling they might have, while respecting that their own experience may be different.

Chiron in the Birth Chart

Here are four questions to ask about the meaning of Chiron in your birth chart:

1. What is your gift to humanity, your method of healing?

2. What do you fear from the outside that seems to do the damage?

3. If your gift is damaged so that you lack confidence, what do you feel as a result?

4. How do you protect yourself from more hurt—what is your survival mode, your self-protection?

With Chiron in each sign, there will be different answers to these four questions. On the next pages are some suggested answers. Do check these thoughts against your own experience and that of other people. Chiron is a relatively recent addition to birth chart readings and its meaning is still being discovered. Your findings are as valid as those of anyone else.

Chiron in Aries

Your gift	1. Encouraging independence
Your fear	2. Other people's lack of faith in you
Your pain	3. Nervousness
Protection	4. Being competitive

Chiron in Taurus

Your gift	1. Steady, physical healing
Your fear	2. Loss of things
Your pain	3. Insecurity
Protection	4. Possessiveness

Chiron in Gemini

Your gift	1. Speaking your truth
Your fear	2. Being misunderstood
Your pain	3. Inability to communicate
Protection	4. Talking too much

Chiron in Cancer

Your gift	1. Emotionally nurturing
Your fear	2. Being neglected
Your pain	3. Feeling that nobody cares
Protection	4. Acting huffy

Chiron in Leo

Your gift	1. Positive, inspiring
Your fear	2. Ridicule
Your pain	3. Feeling that your inner fire has gone out
Protection	4. Hiding or controlling

Chiron in Virgo

Your gift	1. Painstakingly caring for people
Your fear	2. Criticism of mistakes
Your pain	3. Uselessness
Protection	4. Overanalyzing things

Chiron in Libra

Your gift	1. Diplomatic, with integrity
Your fear	2. Rejection
Your pain	3. Loneliness
Protection	4. Trying too hard to please

Chiron in Scorpio

Your gift	1. Deeply understanding
Your fear	2. Emotional attack
Your pain	3. Constantly in emotional pain
Protection	4. Hiding your feelings

Chiron in Sagittarius

Your gift	1. Freeing other people's minds from orthodoxy
Your fear	2. Criticism of ideas
Your pain	3. Fear of freedom
Protection	4. Being argumentative

Chiron in Capricorn

Your gift	1. Fearless handling of changes
Your fear	2. Other people's lack of faith in your ability
Your pain	3. Feeling incompetent, like a victim
Protection	4. Refusing to get involved

Chiron in Aquarius

Your gift	1. Faith in human value
Your fear	2. Being let down or forcibly cut off
Your pain	3. Feeling disillusioned
Protection	4. Feeling cynical

Chiron in Pisces

Your gift	1. Empathic service through merging
Your fear	2. Being swamped or hurt
Your pain	3. Feeling worthless
Protection	4. Being shy

We Are Not Separate from Spirit

Every planet represents a spiritual quality. Qualified through its placement in a Zodiac sign and house, its energy reflects part of the personality. When we harbor the mistaken belief of thinking ourselves separate from our Source, we clutter ourselves with feelings of guilt and fear, the need for attack and defense, and a host of consequent negative feelings.

In feeling separate, we judge our energy to be wrong, shameful, and unacceptable, denying our spirit's acceptance of all that we are. The result is a sense of personality that is divided, with some planets reflecting beautiful virtues and others reflecting "dreadful defects." We set them against each other to do battle within ourselves, seeing their relationships, or aspects, as either good or bad.

What we can do to release ourselves from the battle, both externally and internally, is to accept our world and our personality as they are, and as reflected by the birth chart, always remembering that we *have* a personality, but it is not who we *are*. The consequent relief brings relaxation, which allows the love of life to flow through us, naturally refining the planetary qualities into a bridge to our essential self.

That Self is spirit unbounded, at one with all existence.

four

The Houses

Ways in Which We Are the Same

It is perfectly possible to read a birth chart without knowing the *time* of birth. When we have only the *date* of birth, the astrological information available will be the positions of the planets in their signs, to within a degree or so of accuracy, and their relationships, or aspects, to each other. However, the Moon moves from 12° to 15° (half a sign) every day, so its exact position cannot be determined.

From this information, an astrologer will be able to interpret the style of the person's energy, what they can express well or with difficulty, what their life and relationships feel like on the inside, and the timing of major life shifts to within a year. What will be unknown is the particular areas of life where all this energy expresses itself, whether it is at work or with friends or at home. Also unknown will be the month-by-month timings possible from the precise placement of the Moon.

Knowing the time of birth, we can calculate what sign was rising over the horizon, the Ascendant, as well as the Midheaven, giving us the twelve houses that enable us to place each planetary energy in a specific area of life.

Not many people know the exact time of their birth to the minute; many times are given on the hour or half hour, which seems like an approximation. But my experience is that when a time is given, the chart for that time seems to give the information that is helpful to the person at the time of the reading. If a person feels uncertain of their birth time, a chart can be constructed for the approximate time, and still give a useful interpretation.

A Bit of Astronomy—The Physical Houses

The Earth is perpetually rolling over toward the eastern sky. Each one of us sits on this beautiful ball watching the sky roll overhead, rising in the east. The planets move slowly through their orbits around the Sun, while the Sun occupies a stationary place in the center of its system of planets. The Earth rolls along its orbit around the Sun, turning completely over in about twenty-three hours and fifty-six minutes.

Sitting on the Earth, if we were to watch the stars by night and measure our time by, say, the star Sirius, we would find that Sirius would be due south approximately every twenty-three hours and fifty-six minutes; however, we actually measure our time by watching the Sun. As we have moved each day about one degree further through our orbit around the Sun, the Sun itself appears to us about one degree further through the Zodiac than the previous day; thus the Sun appears to have traveled 361° in the full twenty-four hours of one day on Earth, Earth Time. The circle of Zodiac signs in the sky consists of 360° and is also sometimes spoken of as being "twenty-four hours" round, each sign being "two hours" wide. This circle of "twenty-four hours" is referred to as star time, or Sidereal Time, and is four minutes different from Earth Time. You do not need to know this to read a chart.

Depending on when your spirit "decides" it is right to come out of your earthly mother, the Earth will be at a particular point in her rolling, and a particular part of the sky will be rising over the horizon. If it is night where your mother is, the Sun will be below the Earth, so if a chart is drawn for that moment with the horizon across the middle of the circle, the Sun will be drawn below the line.

To draw the chart, we are looking south, so the rising degree is on the left. The first house begins at that rising point and refers to that area of sky rising next, so it is below the horizon. The second and subsequent houses follow it, and so are numbered counterclockwise.

The Midheaven, or Medium Coeli (MC), is above the horizon. It refers to the degree of the Zodiac belt on the local meridian, that

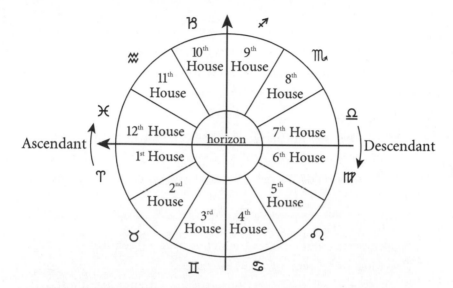

imaginary line from north to south at the chart location. In most systems of house division, the MC begins the tenth house, so all twelve houses derive from the horizon and the local meridian. These two lines cut the chart into four sections, each containing three houses.

The horizon indicates our relationship with what we find around us. The beginning (the cusp) of the first house is called the Ascendant and indicates how we are predisposed to see the world around us, and also our appearance, our behavior or interface with what we see. The Descendant (cusp of the seventh house) indicates what qualities of relationship our behavior attracts in order to balance our Ascendant qualities. The MC (cusp of the tenth house) shows what we see as ideal, and therefore what we reach to achieve for ourselves. The Immum Coeli, or IC (cusp of the fourth house), is the foundation that we stand on to reach those ideals, our early life and sense of security.

The Twelve Houses

The twelve houses divide the full circle of our world, describing what we are looking toward and the different areas of our life experience, as follows (in brackets are the particular relationships that tend to be associated with those areas).

First House

New situations, my appearance, the way others see me.

   (People: Those I am just meeting)

Second House

My possessions, my personal money and income, my immediate environment, the house I live in, my body, the things I value.

   (People: Those I live with, those who occupy the same house)

Third House

Communication with that which is near to me through speech, writing, or movement; local journeys.

   (People: My relatives, siblings, school friends, neighbors)

Fourth House

Home, where I feel at home, my nest, my roots, land.

   (People: The family into which I was born, the least-known parent—tends to be the father)

Fifth House

Creative outlets and ventures, hobbies, recreation, entertainment, pleasure, romance.

   (People: Children, lovers, all creative works)

Sixth House

Routines of daily life, job, work, health, service to others.

   (People: Colleagues, employees, pets, clients, those I serve or who serve me)

Seventh House

My relationship with my world.

(People: My close friends, my partner, my spouse, my "other half," the other person in any one-to-one relationship)

Eighth House

Other people's money, inheritance, shared resources, the underlying rules of relationship, business partnership, ecology of the Earth, opportunities to transform myself through relationships.

(People: Business partners, deeply emotionally close partners, those who challenge my control)

Ninth House

Chosen field of study, higher education, philosophy, religion, the principles by which I was brought up, the law, long journeys, travel.

(People: Teachers, those whose ideas influence me philosophically, religious inspirer, guru, my in-laws)

Tenth House

Vocation, career, public face, reputation, fame.

(People: The best-known parent—tends to be the mother, those with qualities I admire, my boss)

Eleventh House

Society, the world "out there," groups, clubs, the audience, the public.

(People: Open friendships, acquaintances, group spirit)

Twelfth House

The unknown, dreams, institutions, events and personality that come forward into this life directly from past lives.

(People: Unseen companions, guides, those who are absent or hidden, access to the unconscious)

Think of the many concerns, activities, and people in your life, and try to imagine which house would contain each one, through which window you would look to see each one.

Creating Our Experience

Every aspect of our personal life, as we live it day by day, is like a window from our personal experience onto a greater life, life as it really is; but, if we need to look through windows, it is necessary that they be clean. We tend to take for granted that what the eye sees is a true representation of what is there, but the windows have been silting up for many lifetimes. All the negative thoughts people have in relation to an area of life leave their dust and grime on the window until eventually many people find that life is a bit boring and gray; the light of reality can hardly penetrate.

There is a need to clear away some of the results of past personal experience from our vision, and, as we realize this, we begin a cleaning process. This may involve counseling or writing a daily journal so that the little forgotten thoughts get more notice; it is often the *whispering background* to our thinking that gives away our true motives and emotional reactions stemming from childhood experiences and before. We may go to workshops on self-development and begin to peel the onion of the personality to find the gold light in the center. But often the *process* of cleaning takes over our attention. We focus on ourselves and our difficulties, almost forgetting the original desire to see through the windows and let the light in.

What is needed at that point is that we accept what we have discovered about ourselves, instead of trying to get rid of it. We realize that it is only our negative thinking and expectation of failure that makes the windows *seem* dirty. When we change our attitude from negative to positive, playful, or adventuresome, the dust and grime disappear. Our focus naturally shifts from continual thoughts of self to what is actually happening through the window.

The houses in astrology represent those windows on every level of experience. They show the expectations that we have of how the world will be in those areas, what we expect to see. They also show our attitudes to those things, how we feel and what we think about them. A lot may be happening in a particular area of our life, but we tend to experience only the part that we recognize from our expectations. That is to say, we are defining, and even limiting, our experience with our own thinking.

Having realized this, there are two ways we can grow. One way is by cleaning the windows, improving our experiences by being ourselves more positively so that life is more enjoyable. The other way is by changing the focus so that the state of the window doesn't prevent us from seeing what is really there. Then we accept ourselves in the way spirit accepts, which dissolves the negativity, and possibly the window, too. We can do either or both.

Improving experience starts with learning how we are creating the problems. We need to accept what it is that we are doing with our energy, how we are projecting ourselves, and we also need to practice doing things differently using the energy at our disposal. This is learning to use the tool kit of personality more skillfully. It can be done by discovering which of the planetary energies have been judged unacceptable or unattainable, and are therefore projected onto others. We need to see the virtue of each energy and how it can be safely used, and also to realize that we already have the qualities we admire in others. Then we can accept these parts of the personality more easily.

Changing the focus deliberately from the window of perception to what is beyond it requires a shift in personal identity, a spiritual awakening. Because we are spirit in truth, it is always possible in theory to identify with it, but even when we realize this as an idea, it is still necessary to develop the *aware experience* of ourselves as spirit. Realizing it is the first great step, but we start from the awareness of ourselves as individuals, and identifying with spirit completely is to enter the Oneness within which there are no separate entities.

The movement toward the experience of Oneness will be different for different people. For some it may be in stages from a vague awareness of inner guidance to a conscious connection with Higher Self as a guide, later identifying with that Higher Consciousness. For others the process may be an undefined maturing, and for others, different still.

Throughout the process, we develop qualities of feeling that are associated with spiritual awakening: compassion for those who used to irritate us, joy for no apparent reason, a peaceful patience where we would have been tense, and so on. While those feelings are present, we are in touch with that source of all life that is within. However, we may want to work at improving our use of personality at the same time.

Our birth chart helps us know the structure of our chosen personality, which is a good beginning; but the principles of the planets and the Zodiac signs are also pointers to spiritual qualities that we can achieve, so they can be used as keys to focusing beyond the glass. By developing the qualities of planets and signs that are relevant to each house in our chart, we can open those windows on the world in order to see what is really there.

EXERCISE

Practice wondering who people really are, especially when you think you know them.

Ways in Which We Are Different

To open our windows on the world and see what is really there, we need to develop the qualities of planets and signs that are relevant to each house in our individual chart. The way we use the houses to describe our individuality is to look through each house window to see which part of the Zodiac was there at our time of birth.

The sign at the beginning of (on the cusp of) each house gives the most effective description, followed by the chart position of its ruling planet. Any planet within that house will show a part of our energy that is triggered by the concerns of that house.

The Ascendant

Any one of 360° in the circle of twelve Zodiac signs could be rising at any moment for each place on the Earth. One of the signs was rising at the moment you were born, and the degree of that sign exactly on the horizon is called your *Ascendant*. It will reflect your spirit's chosen way of relating to the world you see around you during this lifetime.

That rising sign (Ascendant) is your way of expressing yourself, your approach to new situations; it is the style with which you naturally greet each new person. If, for some reason, it is difficult for you to express that sign, you will not come across very easily at all. It would be like losing the interface of your personality-computer with the user you are trying to meet. That person would look at you, wondering what is going on, and may well lose interest. One way to deal with such a situation is to wait for the first moment to pass and then go straight into using one of the other planetary energies, such as Mercury (speech) or Venus (warm receptivity) instead of assuming that your Ascendant style is the only way in which to express yourself.

Any planet that was rising or was about to rise at your birth will be shown on the Ascendant or in the first house in your birth chart, and represents the nature of the energy that comes across from you in new situations. If that planet is Mars, it indicates an energetic approach in the style of the sign it is in. So if Mars is in Scorpio, it would show that you come across with an emotional intensity in your energy that some people may step back from because they are unsure about whether you are safe to approach. Others who have some of that style in their own nature, and are comfortable with it, are likely to feel attracted to you.

The Ascendant and Descendant in Relationships

In relationships, our different desires and styles of behavior tend to get tangled up with the people to whom we find ourselves relating. Each rising sign is looking for its own ideal person, yet once that person is found, the behavior changes, sometimes dramatically. When facing people to whom we have begun to relate closely, we experience them as having changed from what was originally expressed, but we cannot blame them because intuitively we know that this other behavior is a part of them. We are drawn to relate to people for so many reasons—astrology merely describes what is happening and also, perhaps, the best that can be attained through the relationship, and its purpose. It is my firm conviction that we need to allow relationships to happen, and use astrology to help us with them once they are underway. To choose a partner solely through astrological compatibility is to deny the level of spiritual choice, which may be for reasons necessary for spiritual growth and healing.

The sign of our Ascendant represents the quality of our first approach to life. Interestingly, we tend to desire people who match this sign, while at the same time needing its complement in our relationships; that is, we want a partner who is like us, but are attracted to people who bring us some qualities of the opposite, setting sign, our Descendant. It is as though in wanting to express ourselves (our Ascendant) in the world, we need the world (the partner) to express what complements us (the Descendant). These Descending qualities are our own natural expression when we choose to really relate to another person. The difficulty comes when we don't consciously realize that we need to express these qualities ourselves. In trying to get that complementary support from the other person, we tend to attract the negative experience of the Descending sign. Once we realize that we are the ones who need to express the Descending quality in our relationships, and we choose to do that positively, then we are able to find relationships where the positive qualities of the Descending sign are expressed through the partnership.

Another experience we can have is that people are attracted to our way of coming across, our Ascendant, yet when we are relating more closely, they find that we can be quite the opposite. Both of us may be caught by this surprise, and it may not be conducive to continuing a close relationship.

Ascendant Aries—Descendant Libra. People with Aries rising generally express themselves directly, combatively, and quickly, unaware of how others feel in response to this. But it is not their intention to drive people away. Their hope is that the partner will meet them with their own truth in exchange, and understanding can be achieved. Libra setting shows that what these people want in relationships is an equal exchange and understanding, but the partners they attract through their Descendant may be people who avoid what seems to them like competition. It can feel to Aries rising as though they are driving their energy into a sponge, and without matching feedback they lack the satisfaction of learning about themselves. So the relationship can become uncertain and frustrating for them.

When Aries-rising people learn to seek out and appreciate their partner's point of view, and express their own truth more gently, learning and adaptation are possible, and the relationship becomes more balanced and harmonious.

Ascendant Taurus—Descendant Scorpio. People with Taurus rising generally express themselves cautiously, kindly, and quietly, and appear to be people who are ultimately steady, can be leaned on at any time, and will always support others. They have Scorpio setting, and in relationships they need deep emotional commitment in order to feel safe. However, they tend to attract people who need their steady support to counteract their own turbulent emotions. On an intimate level, deep feelings matter to people with Taurus rising, so their relationships can be stormy, with extreme ups and downs, and because they want stability, they tend to blame their partners for the storms.

People with Taurus rising must learn to express their true feelings in a steady and kind way, so that their partners understand what they really need. A relationship in which deep emotions can be aired without shaking the foundations can become very close and long lasting.

Ascendant Gemini—Descendant Sagittarius. People with Gemini rising generally express themselves lightly, charmingly, and probably verbally, and want to talk with everyone they meet. This will be modified by the natural style of communication indicated by the position of Mercury in their chart. With Sagittarius setting, they like their partnerships to be meaningful and fun. If they express only the Gemini, their chatter is likely to bore the kind of people they want to be with, and they will find their partners drifting to more interesting company, while they themselves tend to be stimulated by new and interesting people.

People with Gemini rising need to pay attention to what is being said, to explore who their partner really is, and listen to the meaning within their words. As they demonstrate real interest in their partner's ideas, the relationship can blossom with creativity and fun, and the stimulation they need will be there for them through that one person.

Ascendant Cancer—Descendant Capricorn. People with Cancer rising generally express themselves emotionally through giving attention, caring, and empathizing. With Capricorn setting, they may look for someone to take care of them, but they tend to find themselves taking responsibility for their partner. The situations that arise force them to fulfill the traditional role they have taken on, and there may be no time for the lighter side of relating, which creates a heavy sense of resentment or burden.

As people with Cancer rising remember to play as well as work, and share the responsibilities of family with their partner as a team, the relationship becomes one of standing side by side, emotionally and practically supporting each other.

Ascendant Leo—Descendant Aquarius. People with Leo rising generally express themselves generously from their heart. They may think they want fun and warmth all the time in relationships, and complain that their Aquarian-style partners, attracted through their Descendant, are cold and distant. People with Leo rising want to be praised rather than needed, and their desire for the partner to be an appreciative audience can put a strain on the relationship, driving the partner away.

In fact, people with Leo rising need space and freedom in relationships to express their radiance in their own special way, in the style of their Sun sign. When they also allow their partners space to be who they are, the appreciation is mutual, and there will be times spent happily together, and other times spent happily apart.

Ascendant Virgo—Descendant Pisces. People with Virgo rising generally express themselves carefully, quietly, and as "perfectly" as they can. They hate to be caught in a mistake because of the criticism they expect, and they direct that sense of high expectation to those to whom they choose to relate. In relationships they try to serve the partner in the way they think is best, assuming that they are the same, which can feel suffocating to the partner. In giving such care, people with Virgo rising can come to expect equal service in exchange, seeing that as a sign of love.

When people with Virgo rising take care of their own needs, and find out what the needs of the partner really are before imposing their own standards, then the partner feels really served. The relationship becomes truly loving and can be spiritually close and romantic.

Ascendant Libra—Descendant Aries. People with Libra rising generally express themselves pleasantly, and are always prepared to follow the general consensus and willing to sacrifice their personal desires for the sake of peace. Aries setting shows an attraction to people who are strong and know their own minds. However, once people with Libra rising are in a close relationship, they become more assertive, having really known what they wanted all along. The person who was originally attracted to them because of the Libran gentleness and apparent flexibility, is suddenly surprised to find that they are not so easygoing after all, wanting to do things their own way.

People with Libra rising need to be honest about what they want, making sure their partner allows them time to come to any decision. The relationship is then between a couple who discuss equally what they will do, with give and take on both sides.

Ascendant Scorpio—Descendant Taurus. People with Scorpio rising generally express themselves in whatever way will distract others from their vulnerability. Their intensity tends to stir up the emotions of others, and they expect deep honesty from anyone "worth" relating to. With Taurus setting, what they are really looking for in a relationship is someone they can rely on, someone who is steady when they themselves are turbulent.

People with Scorpio rising are deeply sensitive to everything in life, and they need to share their vulnerability with their partner. Only when they are prepared to risk hurt by being open will their partner know them well enough to give the support they need. Only when people with Scorpio rising are prepared to commit themselves to a relationship will their partner feel sufficiently safe with them to settle down.

Ascendant Sagittarius—Descendant Gemini. People with Sagittarius rising generally express themselves with interest and enthusiasm, looking for adventure and play in relationships. They tend to be interested in many people and many ideas, and may have a phobia about being pinned down into one relationship in case they get bored. With Gemini setting, it is people who listen to them with interest that keep their attention, when what is equally necessary is that those with Sagittarius rising listen to other people.

As people with Sagittarius rising listen to who their partner really is, they will discover the partner endlessly interesting, just as is every person they meet. As they allow themselves to be happily surprised when finding other people different from what they expected, they will experience a feeling of being alive in all their relationships.

Ascendant Capricorn—Descendant Cancer. People with Capricorn rising generally express themselves seriously and competently, and are cautious of what they take on because they know that their integrity will require them to follow through. People with Capricorn rising have often been overly responsible from childhood, and they may desire their partner to be caring of them like the ideal mother or father. However, they tend to find that they can do things more easily than the partner, so they continue to take full responsibility. Thus the partner is reduced to being a "child" in the relationship.

People with Capricorn rising need to appreciate their partner's way of doing things even when it seems to be more laborious or inefficient. This appreciation for the partner's style provides emotional support while encouraging independent action. In this way, the partner will feel more inclined to offer caring support to them.

Ascendant Aquarius—Descendant Leo. People with Aquarius rising generally express themselves very little during the first encounter, observing the other person and giving little away. Other people see this "poker face" and are either intrigued or repelled by it. Once the other person is accepted or known, the Leo Descendant of Aquarius rising expresses as humor and warmth, but is careful not to upset the partner due to a fear of rejection. Such warmth and concern can produce a relationship where each person becomes dependent on the other for producing the sunshine in their life, but people with Aquarius rising abhor dependency. They are likely to cool off and detach, leaving the partner clinging to a memory of warmth, and maybe trying to recreate it by force.

When people with Aquarius rising are prepared to be completely honest in their day-to-day relating, taking space when they need it without worrying about the partner's reaction, the relationship can develop into one of great integrity and friendship as well as warmth and passion.

Ascendant Pisces—Descendant Virgo. People with Pisces rising generally express themselves in the mood of the moment without recognizing what they are putting out. They are so sensitive to the emotions around them that they are likely to reflect back to a person the mood that person is trying to hide. They are looking for a partner who expresses the human ideals that they try themselves to personify. With Virgo setting, this can be a tall order, and people with Pisces rising find that every relationship falls short at some point. Their partners can find it impossible to simply be themselves without hurting or offending the Pisces-rising person's sensitivities.

People with Pisces rising need to realize that all people are struggling to be the best they can be, although they do not always succeed. Tolerance of human frailties in themselves and others expresses as compassion, and the Virgo Descendant expresses as assistance and support in relationships. In demonstrating such service to each other, the couple serves us all.

We are often confused about what we need in relationships. The planet that often confuses us is Venus, the energy of attraction. Venus reflects the energy we feel comfortable with when actively relating to people, and the style of affection we like to receive.

However, what we want is not always what we need, and it is much more worthwhile in terms of general happiness to uncover what we need and develop that. The Venus qualities will continue anyway as part of the chemistry of our relationships. Our need for a complement expressed by the Descendant is a large background issue.

For example, someone who has Leo rising, and therefore Aquarius setting, and also Venus in Pisces will have a need in relationships for the space expressed by the Descending sign of Aquarius, even though the Venus in Pisces may reflect a romantic desire for merging with the partner. In this case it is the space that is most important in order for a relationship to survive. Constant merging would stifle both partners, but occasional romantic interludes could add the excitement that an Aquarius relationship thrives on.

Our Relationship with the World

We are all predisposed to see things in a certain way that is individual to our specific past experience and our faculties of perception and interpretation. From a personality point of view, it is our expectation of what we will see through the windows that determines what we actually see. It follows that, when we look at our experiences in the world, what we are seeing is a reflection of our personality. So we will now examine the houses in these two ways: first, how our attitudes and expectations create our experience; and second, how our experience reflects our personality.

It is the Zodiac sign at the beginning (on the cusp) of each house that shows our attitude to that part of our world. The sign on the cusp is the primary indicator of how we feel about that area of life, what kind of experiences we expect when engaged in those activities, and therefore what we actually experience as happening to us. Our life will be this way because this is the way we expect it to be.

Wonderfully, once we know this, we can begin to let go of our expectations and become prepared to be surprised.

The Houses: How Our Attitudes and Expectations Create Our Experience

The sign on the cusp of a house in our own chart, and the chart position of the planet ruling that sign, show our attitude to the concerns of that house. They show how we expect our experience to be in that area of life (active energy), and what we see coming back to us (passive perception). In each case, our perceived experience will confirm our suspicions. In the following section, an example is given in parentheses for each house with a particular sign on the cusp. In practice, the cusp of the first house could be in any sign.

First House

Our attitude toward ourselves, how we expect to be when facing life; what life looks like to us. (*e.g., Scorpio:* "I am vulnerable when I approach life—life hurts me, in the area where Pluto is.")

Second House

Our attitude toward the physical world in general, what we feel we deserve, what we receive by way of earnings, what we value about ourselves. (*e.g., Leo:* "I enjoy my possessions—my income describes my worth through the Sun's house activity; I value my self-expression in the Sun's house.")

Third House

Our attitude toward learning and communication, how we expect people to talk, how we see people reacting to us. (*e.g., Libra:* "Speech should be diplomatic—people like relating to me about the concerns of the Venus house.")

Fourth House

Our attitude toward our early life, how we expect our home to be, how our father seemed to be. (*e.g., Sagittarius:* "My home is interesting—my father was fun in Jupiter-house ways.")

Fifth House

Our attitude toward creativity in ourselves and others, what we expect from love affairs and from children, how affairs pan out, how children behave with us. (*e.g., Gemini:* "I have fun with words and storytelling; variety triggers my creativity; I talk to children as equals—children chat to me about things of Mercury's house.")

Sixth House

Our attitude toward the routines of life and our health, what we expect our working conditions to be, the kind of jobs we get, what affects our health. (*e.g., Capricorn:* "It is important to be organized—I get responsible jobs in the field of Saturn's house.")

Seventh House

Our attitude toward our partner or spouse and how we expect them to behave, the issues we seem to have to deal with in relationships, how our partner seems to be. (*e.g., Pisces:* "My partner should know how I feel—we are so intuitive, especially about Neptune-house concerns.")

Eighth House

Our attitude toward other people's values and possessions, what we expect to get from any important partnership, power struggles. (*e.g., Aquarius:* "Equality of ownership—clear rules about freedom in the issues of Uranus' house.")

Ninth House

Our attitude toward life, religion, study, and teaching; how we expect teachers to be; the way we gather knowledge and understanding of life. (*e.g., Virgo:* "People should help each other—I study hard in the house of Mercury.")

Tenth House

Our attitude toward our career and our top priorities, the results we expect when going for our ideals, what happens when we do our best, how our mother seems to be. (*e.g., Taurus:* "A career should be safe—I succeed if I relate in the Venus house.")

Eleventh House

Our attitude toward groups of people and toward society, how we expect to be treated in group situations, the way the world seems to treat us, what happens when we identify with a group. (*e.g., Aries:* "Each person in a group should be responsible for themselves—my contribution will be what I want to do in the Mars house.")

Twelfth House

Our attitude toward the unknown and toward being alone, what we expect to be missing in the world around us, what we seem to be without in childhood and have to find within ourselves. (*e.g., Cancer:* "Being on my own is nurturing—I meditate when I am involved in the activities of the house that contains the Moon.")

EXERCISE

Practice imagining the attitude of different signs on the cusp of each house.

"By accepting myself as I am, and the world and people around me as my reflection, my struggle with life fades. As I relax, I enjoy my life more, and the reflection gently becomes nearer to what I would like it to be; my experience changes."

The Houses: How Our Experience Reflects Our Personality

The sign on the cusp and the chart position of the planet ruling that sign show how I feel I am, and need to be, in order to meet the challenges of that house well. If I can accept that my personality equipment is like this, and allow myself to express these qualities, a great deal of struggle and difficulty goes out of my life immediately, and other people will accept me as I feel myself to be. If I allow my personality to be the way it prefers, I relax, and others relax around me and are more easily able to be themselves, too.

In the next section, the examples of signs on the house cusps are the same as used previously, showing how each attitude *feels* to the person who has it.

First House

Who I think I am, my way of approaching the world, which is reflected in what the world seems to be about. (*e.g., Scorpio on the cusp:* Sensitive at a deep level; "I need to approach life this way.")

Second House

How I feel about myself, my sense of worth, what I value in myself, which is reflected in what the world pays me for what I do. *(e.g., Leo on the cusp:* Positivity and fun; "I need to feel that these qualities are valuable.")

Third House

How I communicate, my way of interacting, which is reflected in the way people react when I speak. *(e.g., Libra on the cusp:* Gently, pleasantly; "I need to communicate things in this way.")

Fourth House

My private face, childhood impressions, and fundamental emotional security, which is reflected in my home life. *(e.g., Sagittarius on the cusp:* Reasons why; "I need this to feel secure.")

Fifth House

My sense of enjoyment, my self-expression as creative, how I play, which is reflected in my creations. *(e.g., Gemini on the cusp:* Communication; "I need this to feel happy.")

Sixth House

My feelings about organizing my daily life, how I "get it together," which is reflected in my health and in my work situation. *(e.g., Capricorn on the cusp:* A sensible work situation; "I need this in order to be organized.")

Seventh House

What I feel I don't have, and thus what I need another person to supply, which is reflected in the behavior of my partner toward me. *(e.g., Pisces on the cusp:* Letting my feelings flow; "I need to be this way in close relationships.")

Eighth House

My depths, my efforts to transform in relation to others, my desire for control and autonomy in deep relationships, which is reflected in people's reactions to me when I reveal my depths. *(e.g., Aquarius on the cusp:* With detachment; "I need to treat my deepest issues this way.")

Ninth House

My sense of meaning and purpose, my search for a map or for guidelines, which is reflected in my teachers. *(e.g., Virgo on the cusp:* Precise; "I need these kinds of guidelines.")

Tenth House

My highest priorities, what I desire the world to acknowledge in me, what I desire to achieve, which is reflected in those I admire. *(e.g., Taurus on the cusp:* My stability; "I need to feel appreciated for this.")

Eleventh House

How I feel about the world, how I see myself in relation to everyone out there, which is reflected in the groups I join. *(e.g., Aries on the cusp:* Independence, directness; "I need to express these qualities in groups.")

Twelfth House

My inner world, my atmosphere, what I search for outside myself and fail to find, what I am blended with so fully that I have difficulty identifying it, which is reflected in my meditation experiences and in my dreams. *(e.g., Cancer on the cusp:* Kind and loving; "I need to connect with this kind of inner guidance.")

EXERCISE

These examples used the same signs as the previous list. Using the signs you put on the cusps in the last exercise, remember the attitude of each sign you used and imagine how a person with that attitude would feel.

My personality molds the way I see life. My mistake is to think that life really is the way I perceive it to be. Sometimes, in the midst of my reactions to what I perceive as happening to me, I can have a quiet, inner sense that things are not what they seem. In that inner part of myself, I recognize that the people I am reacting to are actually just being themselves, and they may not mean what I think they mean. At this point I can begin to have a living relationship with the world as it is, and not just with my thoughts and feelings about it.

Planets in the Houses

Any planet in a house shows the energy we put directly into those concerns, and also the way we experience them. For instance:

a) Uranus in the seventh house may say, "I want to be free in relationships." The experience tends to be of relating to someone who is not there much of the time, or of many changes in relationship.

b) An uncomfortably aspected Saturn in the fifth house may say, "I'm not old enough or stable enough to handle the responsibility of having children." These people would be very likely to leave the disciplining to their spouse; when they have to take charge, they would tend to compensate for their sense of weakness by being overly controlling.

c) Venus in the tenth house may say, "I want everybody to love me." They present attractiveness to the world, pleasant manners, social aptitude, and the world loves them.

d) Jupiter in the second house says, "Money? Easy come, easy go!" They experience little problem in earning enough for their needs, maybe much more, spending or giving away all that they get.

Here is a little about each planet in relation to its effect on the house it occupies in a birth chart.

☉ *The Sun*

The house that contains the Sun in a chart is of prime importance. Bearing in mind that the Sun represents our central self, and allows the spirit entry into everyday life, it is necessary not only to be our Sun sign, but also to be active in the house where it is located.

The Sun in Capricorn in the third house indicates people who need not only to express competence and serious carefulness, but also to express it in words to other people.

The Sun in Aquarius in the second house describes people who have the welfare of all members of society at heart, and who also need to be paid for working in that field, if they are to value themselves.

The latter example is the kind of situation where people can negate their sense of worthiness as individuals, because their principles seem to deny what they personally need. It is here that knowing their birth chart can be such a relief, because it will validate their own needs so that they are able to see the principle in perspective.

The people relevant to the house containing the Sun (listed at the beginning of this chapter) are the ones to whom we tend to give our light away, so that they become the source of light and life, we fall in love, give our heart away, etc.:

The Sun in the fifth house does this to the lover or the child;

The Sun in the sixth house, to the client;

The Sun in the second house, to the acquisition of possessions;

The Sun in the ninth house, to the teacher or religious leader.

When we do this, that person's opinion can make or break us, we feel we cannot live without them, and we need to draw back that power. Being and appreciating ourselves in the area of life of the Sun's house helps us achieve that return of the light to our own heart center, where it has to be.

☽ *The Moon*

The house that contains the Moon is the area of life where we have the natural talent of the Moon's sign and are automatically involved. We assume that everyone else will feel the same, unless another planet brings this area of life into our consciousness.

The Moon in the eighth house indicates people who will always react to the deepest level of life situations. That reaction may be light conversation about a situation if the Moon is in Gemini, or seeing the positive or funny side of a situation if the Moon is in Leo. Their mother may have had that perspective herself, which would have been part of the attraction for this particular spirit to be the child, so that the characteristic would be embedded in the upbringing. People with an eighth-house Moon tend to take it for granted that those around them are involved in deep issues; how the Moon is aspected will show whether they like that or not.

The Moon near the Descendant or in the seventh house may show as an assumption of being in relationship with everyone to whom they are near. Sometimes these people forget to say anything to their companion because they do not feel the need to do so. Other people may find this a bit offhand, but when anyone makes the effort to connect with these people, they find them immediately receptive.

☿ *Mercury*

The house containing Mercury is the area of life that most often gets the spotlight of our conscious attention. The issues of this house will be the subjects that provoke our thought, and we are therefore more likely to want to learn about them. As we think, so we communicate, and conversations are likely to come back to these areas. Where Mercury is, we want to understand, which tends to result in us focusing on the problems of that area.

Mercury in the eighth house indicates people with the mentality of a detective, always trying to get to the bottom of things. If Mercury is in Taurus, they will look at the depths in a practical way, perhaps aiming to find a practical solution; if in Libra, they may examine situations with a view to establishing harmony.

In the twelfth house, Mercury tends to think best when alone, which makes writing a comfortable way to communicate. Conscious understandings can arise from dreams, or in meditation, if these people are open to learning this way.

♀ *Venus*

We tend to express our personal love in the area of the Venus house. We want to be in relationship in those specific activities, and we feel loved when people appreciate our efforts there. Because we are likely to express our lovelier behavior there, we tend to have more contact with people when we are involved in the activities of that house.

People with Venus in the tenth house will attract people when occupied with their career, which will need to involve others. In the ninth house, people will be the focus when traveling or studying favorite subjects. With Venus in the fourth house, people will be attracted to their home. When Venus is in the twelfth house, relationships may be idealized or spiritual; these people are more loved than they realize.

Uncomfortable aspects to Venus will show as relationship difficulties when the person is involved in the activities of the house or houses ruled by Venus. Venus in the sixth house could manifest as a tendency to have trouble with colleagues, or maybe a health problem connected to the throat; in the second house, perhaps recurring problems with those living in the same house and sharing possessions.

Whatever the house, the problems can be sorted out only by the people themselves working on understanding the principle of love. That love attracts and receives, it does not take or possess.

♂ *Mars*

We tend to energize those situations that relate to the Mars house. Mars in the seventh house shows in dynamic relationships; in the ninth house, in the energetic pursuit of learning or travel, depending on the sign and aspects.

When we looked at planets in signs, one of the useful exercises was to check the position of Mars for clues to give us methods for triggering our energy when we need it. Using the houses as well as signs gives us more information, because the house placement of Mars shows the area of activity that fires our energy for action.

For instance, Mars in the fifth house may describe people who need to feel they have room to be creative; and when life becomes repetitive they will have no energy at all. To get energy flowing, they will need to discover or create an enjoyable side to their work.

However, Mars in the sixth house will simply find that the energy flows when work is there to be done. Mars in the twelfth may find that they are better working on their own; whereas in the seventh they will need company every now and then to keep the flow going, even if that company is just a telephone call.

♃ *Jupiter*

The house containing Jupiter will be an area where we grow and expand easily from an early age. If we are not engaged in any activity relating to this house, we will feel stunted and blocked, giving rise to depression, frustration, or illness, whichever is our personal response. Activating the Jupiter house brings a breath of fresh air into our life, with a sense of greater possibilities and a straightforward pleasure in life.

People with Jupiter in the twelfth house need to be involved in some kind of inner work, where they will meet the Jupiter as a guardian-angel energy; there will be great pleasure derived from time alone.

Jupiter in the tenth house may indicate people who make a career of their job by giving unstintingly, and their efforts will be reflected by an approving boss. It could also indicate people who dare to follow their vocation instead of just seeking steady employment, who then receive the gratitude of all those who benefit from their efforts.

When we carry out, in any house containing Jupiter, those expansive activities where the focus is on the activity rather than on ourselves, Jupiter is reflected back to us as encouragement and opportunities to expand in the field of that house and any of the houses connected to Jupiter by aspect.

♄ *Saturn*

The house containing Saturn is that area of life where we feel a serious need to be in control; it is the same area where we received the discipline of authority figures in childhood. We are liable to blame the people relevant to that house for the testing times we have there, but many of the tests are difficult only if we have not been doing the necessary work beforehand. Once we accept that we are largely creating our own difficulties, we come to understand what is really happening. The inner developmental work results in a wisdom and natural authority that other people will accept and appreciate.

For instance, Saturn in the ninth house shows first as a fairly rigid set of rules in childhood, an ideology that was expressed as a fixed truth. Later, these people will need to examine their assumptions about life, or they may continue to limit themselves in the same way their parents did. People with a ninth-house Saturn may well choose to follow a course of study that they take very seriously, and eventually, because Saturn generally unfolds slowly in life, they could find themselves sharing the chosen subject with others. If they have been through the process of disciplining their own study and discovering their own truth, they could be good, patient teachers.

The early life of people with Saturn in the third house will show some kind of restriction in spontaneous talking, possibly a difficult school life, or an absence of someone to talk to. Later, as they learn communication skills, they will need to accept that they sound authoritative when they speak, and they will naturally take responsibility for what they say.

If Saturn has any connection with the fifth house, it brings a perseverance to creativity that enables works of art to be manifested. This is relevant to all serious artistic endeavors.

♅ *Uranus*

The house placement of Uranus shows us in what area of life we will tend to feel trapped, and therefore behave in ways that result in a sense of freedom.

Uranus in the sixth house reflects people who need freedom in their working life, and if it is not part of their job, they may well keep changing employment, or work for themselves. It is clear that the most suitable kind of work would need to include an amount of independent choice or the use of initiative, or even movement from place to place, depending on the sign Uranus occupies and how it fits with the rest of the chart.

We bring into our Uranus house an energy of excitement and the unexpected that other people are not sure how to handle. We avoid predictability in order to remain unattached. Maintaining a certain detachment in that area of life enables us to have flashes of insight into what is really happening.

Uranus in the third house indicates people who may keep quiet much of the time, and then surprise everyone with words that may well be enlightening, or may simply be meant to shock.

♆ *Neptune*

We are particularly open in the areas of the house Neptune occupies; psychic or spiritual connection is a possibility through the activities related to this house. We can experience confusion in the matters of this house until we dedicate those activities to a higher purpose, rather than simply focusing on the personal.

Neptune in the first house indicates people who go forward in life, dissolving the form of what they approach. They need to see the essence within people and share in the oneness of spirit in order not to be swamped by the merging process.

To have Neptune near the IC or in the fourth house can feel like standing on sand as the tide comes in, very uncertain, vague, and insecure, unless and until these people realize that they are very sensitive, spiritual people. In the same way that we need a steady chair to stand on to reach up and change a light bulb, we need to stand on a well-rooted IC to reach for and achieve the MC, which is the expression of our ideal in the world. Once these people have made spirituality the cornerstone of their life, they are on a secure rock, and all the rest of life becomes easier.

♇ *Pluto*

Pluto, in its house position, shows the issues that seem most important. For people who have Pluto near the Ascendant or in the first house, all life feels intensely important. Their fear tends to attract powerful and difficult situations, and they incur a great deal of needless suffering in their endeavor to survive the dangers they perceive at every turn. Since other people tend to find this attitude disconcerting, they often have to deal with their difficulties alone.

What they need to know is that life is important but need not be that dangerous, that our spirit only ever presents us with what we can manage, and wants only for us to grow into a state where we can better enjoy life. Pluto in this position indicates that these people are capable of the great self-transformation that is required to let go of their fearful controlling. In such a climate of deep change, the people around them are also able to transform.

Pluto in the tenth or eleventh house indicates people who feel a need to change the world in some way. It will be attended by a fear of doing just that and, consequently, a manner that is so intense that they can easily attract opposition or rejection. But there are times and situations that call for such people to initiate changes in human behavior.

⚷ *Chiron*

The house placement of Chiron describes the activities we lack confidence to engage in right from childhood. It can be read as the wound we were born with, as though in a past life we died of it, and so it is often seen in people as great vulnerability when they are involved with the concerns of the house it occupies.

In the eleventh house, Chiron may describe people who would like to help society, their country, or a particular group. They may also feel that people will not trust them, will belittle or misunderstand their efforts, and so they will have experienced putdowns that were not necessarily intended. There is likely to be a lack of confidence that, to others, seems quite unfounded. As they come to realize that their input is often welcome and trusted because it is valuable, the desire to help overcomes their anxiety, and they become catalysts for healing in whatever way suits the sign.

People who have Chiron in the seventh house are wounded in the area of partnership. Because they tend to be attracted to people who are going to hurt them, even unwittingly, they need to realize that other people can also be hurt. As they stretch out to care for others, relationships become the field of change and healing for both parties.

Ruling Planets of "Empty" Houses

The concerns of a house trigger the flow of energy of the planet it contains, and that flow creates activity. When a house doesn't contain any planets, those concerns do not of themselves spark activity. The area in life that we tap for the energy to handle those activities will be the house containing the ruling planet of the sign on the cusp. Here are some guidelines for analyzing "empty" houses:

1. Look for the sign on the cusp of the house that you are studying; this sign will show the attitude to that particular area of life.

2. Look for the house position of the planet ruling that sign. That planet's sign and house will show the supporting energy the person can use for the house you are studying.

For example, suppose you are wondering about family, and the sign on the fourth-house cusp is Virgo. These people's attitude to home and family will be reflected by Virgo, probably helpful but also cool and analytical; there is also likely to be a tendency toward self-criticism, which will affect their emotional security. Mercury is the ruler of Virgo, so if, for example, Mercury is in the first house, these

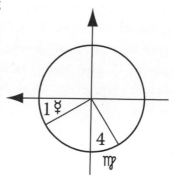

people will tend to talk about their home, family, and early life as soon as you meet them, which might very well help them understand their inner feelings. If Mercury was in Gemini, we would expect the flow of talking to be emphasized; the aspects to Mercury will show if this is a comfortable thing for them to do or not.

Next, imagine you are looking for the best kind of subject for a person to study, and you find Pisces on the cusp of the ninth house; you might say that the attitude toward learning will be rather vague, unless they pursue spiritual or religious studies. If the ruler of Pisces, Neptune, is in the eleventh house, they are more likely to feel attracted to a course if they will be studying with a group with whom they will feel a sense of bonding. If Neptune is in the fifth house, the subject they 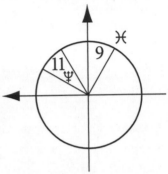 choose to study might well be more artistic and creative, and they might be more comfortable studying on their own.

Looking at the twelfth house, you might wonder what form of meditation would be most likely to appeal to a person. If the cusp of this house is in Taurus, you might suggest meditating in nature, with trees, or the person imagining that they are a tree for strength and stability. If Venus, the ruler of Taurus, is in the sixth house, it might be easier and thus more appropriate for the person to develop a meditative state when working. We would expect their work to involve relating to 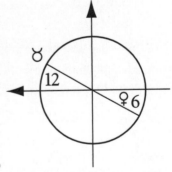 people (Venus), and they would feel more motivated to meditate (twelfth house) for help and information about their clients (sixth house).

EXERCISE

1. Take a house that interests you in your own chart or a friend's chart and look at the sign on its cusp. What does it tell you about those issues or activities?

2. Find the position in the chart of the ruler of that sign.

3. Expand your thinking about the original house to include the interests of the ruler's house.

4. Notice the difference.

Looking Beyond the "Windows"

By now it should be clear that there is no cause to think that we know what makes people tick, what moves them, what their priorities are. People are so complex that it would take years of patient study to cover all their character possibilities; and they are growing and changing all the time, whereas any piece of knowledge is static. Do we ever really know even our own personality? What is personality, anyway? For each of us, our world is so personal, yet we would like to know what is really out there.

The point of this questioning is to reach a state of not knowing who we all are, even our friends and family. In this way, we are open to seeing each other as individuals who are constantly changing, and we will be nearer to true relating than any amount of knowledge could bring us. The study of our birth charts gives us clues to those differences that we miss due to our unconscious assumptions: "Surely everyone is like that!" we say of some characteristic we take for granted in ourselves.

This study also helps us approach a relationship difficulty or the struggle to make a decision. One of the most valuable benefits of contact with our birth chart is the confirmation of our feeling about ourselves, so that we are better able to accept our personality and not try to make it into something it cannot be. Perhaps, through that growing acceptance, we will become able to truly know ourselves in the greatest sense, and to encompass what is beyond our "windows" on the world.

✿ ✿ five ✿ ✿

The Nodes of the Moon

Ways in Which We Are the Same

Our Story

The Nodes of the Moon seem to tell our story from before this life, through the present and into what we make of our potential. It is not that we leave our past behind; we never do that. We *are* our past; that is what we are made of, and so we bring it with us. The Nodes show how our ability to accept all that we are is the necessary first step toward the direction that attracts us. When going in that direction, there is a satisfaction that makes life feel worth living. We feel, "That's what I want to be doing!" Even if we have difficulty with it, we still feel it is right for us. When we follow our own Nodal path, there is a feeling of determination, strength, and rightness that goes beyond the everyday ups and downs of life.

The more we are aware of the oneness that we are in truth, the less we experience measurable time. Our spirit, previewing this life, seeing the way things are and the processes and changes that will be happening in the world, recognizes the appropriate time to be born. Scanning this life from that other dimension, looking for the time best suited to our arrival, we, as spirit, would consider what might be achievable in an earthly life, whether we could be helpful to the world, or learn to improve our own experience.

We may consider what attributes we are going to need from the many lifetimes we have lived before. If we had spent an entire lifetime working to develop certain attributes, an intuitive aspect of the imagination, for instance, or some practical skills, we would have become very good at them. In order to do this, we would have needed to concentrate on a specific area of experience, and because we can't be aware of everything all the time, we would naturally have developed habits that enabled us to focus on that area. What we have been working on becomes a talent, a skill, so the habit patterns, stored in the unconscious, will kick in whenever the skill is next used.

We may have developed an infinite number of skills through many experiences, but we bring in only those that are relevant to this life. As it becomes clear which skills are relevant, we collect them, and along with them come the old habits, attitudes, assumptions, and any unsolved problems left over from those lifetimes. These could include difficulties like a relationship that was not resolved, an accident that occurred for which we were responsible, or maybe the end of a life where we had no time to integrate the experiences around that particular death.

Our chosen character manifests at our birth as a conglomerate of bits of personality, all described by the arrangement of the planets at the time. That group of personality tools is all to be combined and used in this life. In the chart, we look at the way the planets are linked together. Those planets that have a comfortable relationship with each other show the skills; and uncomfortable relationships, shown by the presence of difficult angles, indicate conflicting parts of ourselves. When astrologers are reading a birth chart, they tend to see many different bits of character, all in the one person; we are all split personalities! During this life we endeavor to integrate the bits so that life is more pleasant.

As we come into this lifetime, behind us is our past, a sense of what we understand and expect. In front of us is the quality and area of life that calls us to achieve, not something specific, but rather an understanding or an expansion of our qualities. The past is represented by the South Node of the Moon, but our direction is toward the opposite point in the Zodiac, the North Node. If we are to speak of the Nodes without referring to past lives, we would say that the South Node shows what feels most natural to us, what we expect.

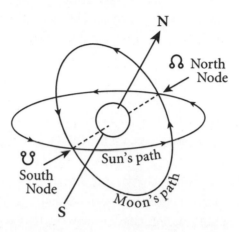

Astronomically speaking, we are looking from the Earth's point of view at the two great circles of the Sun and Moon. If you were to watch the Sun from the center of the Earth, you would see it move through all the signs of the Zodiac during the year, making a circle around the Earth called the *ecliptic*. The Moon's path takes only four weeks to complete and is at a different angle. Those two circles intersect at opposite points in the Zodiac called the Moon's Nodes with the Sun. Where the Moon was about to go south of the Sun's path is the South Node, and the North Node is where the Moon was moving to the north of the Sun's path. Because the Moon represents the automatic personality, when contrasted with the Sun as the spirit, the Moon's Nodes speak to us of the role of the personality for the spirit.

We gathered our personality to do something in this life, and the Nodes give us a clue as to what that might be. They are sometimes called the Head and Tail of the Dragon; the person whose chart it is being the Dragon with their own Head facing the North Node and their Tail caught up in the South Node. It is as though we have a map of the land we have already explored, perhaps our last earthly experience before this life, shown by the sign and house that contains our South Node. That kind of behavior feels familiar and therefore gives a sense of security, but, being out of date, it can create painful experiences.

In contrast, where we are going is unknown. We want to be there, but we tend to feel apprehensive or tentative about that area of our life (the house containing the North Node) and about behaving in that way (its sign). This is because it is the direction our spirit has chosen, and the personality senses that it will need to reach beyond itself to go that way. In the new land, we have no map. Even though other people may find that kind of thing easy, we feel insecure there, no matter how much advice we get.

However, people often charge into life determined to go toward the North Node immediately, trying to do that sign and house where the North Node falls in their chart, whenever they are feeling adventurous, or reckless. They manage it for a while, but their lack of experience and skill in that area makes it is difficult to maintain. Things go wrong, mistakes are made, and they tend to fall back into the South Node habits and assumptions because at least that is simple, even though not what they really want. Hopefully, we learn a little more with each attempt, understanding what is required of us as we improve contact with our spirit.

Off the Path and Getting Back On

Sometimes, at an early age, people decide that the North Node area is too painful. They stop trying to achieve it and either carry on in the old ways, which become less and less acceptable to them, or they lose their direction altogether.

Not being on our Nodal path feels like being lost: "What am I here for?" "What am I supposed to be doing?" Nothing else that we attempt gives us that feeling of satisfaction. Inside we feel a sense of yearning that we may not even be able to define. When the North Node type of experience is spoken of, we feel, "If only I could . . ." That longing can poison life.

The reason for this failure to achieve the North Node is that the tools we brought with us to do that job are on the step we came in on, shown by the South Node. To get back on the path, it is necessary to look again at the South Node area of life to see what was important. We need to become aware of the habits that hold us back from development.

Habits of behavior and attitude are areas of unconsciousness that need to be unlocked. They are just functions relevant to the past, and left to run on their own. Every now and then it is a good idea to examine our habits and bring them up to date, so that they are useful and do not hold us back. We need to correct our responses to situations so that they are appropriate in the moment.

We also need to respect ourselves for the abilities that we do have, rather than regard them as universal, thinking that "surely everybody can do that," or even seeing them as weaknesses, as in the case of emotional sensitivity. Sometimes we have to relearn the skills or knowledge of the past, but we will always find that they come naturally, which suggests that we knew them before and are now remembering them again. All these are necessary tools to help us at every step.

It is also important to recognize that other people may not have our South Node abilities. When we use them only unconsciously, or for our own benefit, we lock ourselves into that personality, and the evolving force of life becomes uncomfortable. But if we use our South Node abilities to benefit others in whatever way feels natural to us, our spirit is expressed and our North Node expression attracts success.

The direction we are facing will be shown by the house and sign that contain our North Node, the Head of our Dragon. It will be the best of that sign that attracts us, and those ideals need to be held in mind like guiding stars, rather than as expectations of immediate achievement. As the South Node is sorted out, the untangling of the Dragon's Tail, we find that the North Node activities and behavior naturally unfold as long as we hold to those ideals. Our efforts to grow in this way attract the help we need to teach us how it is to be done. In a nutshell, when we have sorted out the step we are on, the next step appears of itself.

The Twelve Directions

The Nodes of the Moon travel slowly backward through the Zodiac, taking nineteen years to complete a cycle. In an ephemeris, only the North Node position is given, the South Node always being directly opposite. It is much more interesting to read about the Nodes if you know where they were when you and your friends were born, so this diagram shows the dates on which the North Node moved backward from one sign into the previous sign. Only the month is given, so you will need to check an ephemeris, in a bookstore perhaps, to find the exact date on which the changeover happened.

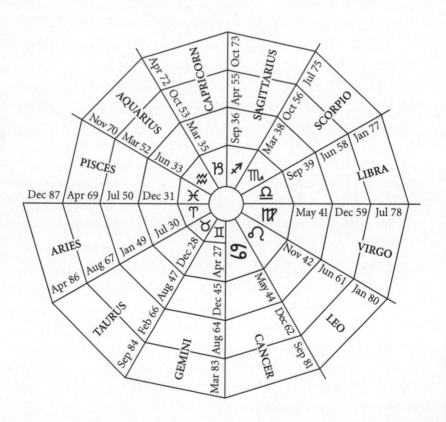

We will be looking at the signs opposite each other. The North Node is in the sign and house that you came into Earth "facing," so you have behind you the sign and house directly opposite.

To describe the **South Node ☋**, or where a person has "come from," we will look for:

1. *Skills* and abilities of sign and house, and;
2. Undermining *habits* of sign and house.

To describe the **North Node ☊**, where and how a person wishes to be active, we will look for:

1. The *ideals* of sign and house, and;
2. *Mistakes* a beginner might make in that sign and house.

☋ ♈ *South Node in Aries (ruler: Mars)*

Skills—Independence, ability to take care of themselves, can operate on own initiative, good at knowing their own way.

Habits—They never ask for help or company because they think no one will help them, they assume they must "go it alone."

☊ ♎ *North Node in Libra (ruler: Venus)*

Ideal—To be in a relationship; expanding self to include the other.

Mistake—Putting the other person first and forgetting their own needs, which leads to frustration, and finally pulling out of, or losing, the relationship; losing the self.

What these people need to remember is that they can manage on their own if necessary, and also that they need a little space to be themselves, so that there is not the need to cling so hard to the relationship. They need to stop pushing people away as soon as the relationship gets difficult. With a little more of the Aries courage, they will dare to risk putting forward *their* point of view as well as the partner's, so that the Libran scales can set about balancing. The conclusions reached will then be less likely to frustrate them, and they will be nearer their Libran ideal of a harmonious relationship.

☋ ♉ *South Node in Taurus (ruler: Venus)*

Skills—Sensed understanding of nature, steady and reliable, natural physical healing ability.

Habits—Stubborn fixity, thinking that time and silence heal all problems.

☊ ♏ *North Node in Scorpio (rulers: Pluto, Mars)*

Ideal—Deep emotional understanding and connectedness.

Mistake—Stirring up emotions unnecessarily, and blaming others for their own huge emotional reactions.

These people need to look toward their Taurus connection with nature, rather than toward their relationships, to gain stability in their life. They will benefit from the silent acceptance of Nature, which will produce the steady, healed state that feels safe to them. From that basis they feel strong enough to speak of their hurt feelings gently, without needing to blame others, so they can attain more readily the Scorpio ideal of deep emotional sharing.

☋ ♊ *South Node in Gemini (ruler: Mercury)*

Skills—Communication, ability to please by recognizing and using other people's styles and language.

Habits—Tendency to talk rather than listen, so nothing is learned, being superficially pleasant and therefore not being trusted by others.

☊ ♐ *North Node in Sagittarius (ruler: Jupiter)*

Ideal—To understand the whole picture, to have an overview of life.

Mistake—Trying to talk about things not yet understood, settling for a superficial overview without the facts to base it on.

These people need to listen with all their Gemini charm in order to find the pieces that go together to make the Sagittarian picture of the whole. Speaking to people in their own language, the style they understand, will draw these people out to speak of what interests them, and the philosophical breadth of conversation will come naturally. In this way these people build their own philosophy of life.

☊ ♋ *South Node in Cancer (ruler: the Moon)*

Skills—Emotional sensitivity, a sense of what will nurture, of how to care for someone.

Habits—Identifying with the child's view of having no control in life, wanting to be cared for.

☋ ♑ *North Node in Capricorn (ruler: Saturn)*

Ideal—To be able to handle any practical situation effectively, to achieve practical aims.

Mistake—Taking responsibility for other people instead of simply for themselves and their own experience.

These people are likely to feel that responsibility is too heavy for them, and the result would be a sense of failure. They need to learn how to care for themselves, giving respect to their own emotional reactions. The caring they then give to others will be more understanding, coming from this position of growing strength. They become able to take on responsible positions without feeling small or emotionally overburdened.

☊ ♌ *South Node in Leo (ruler: the Sun)*

Skills—Positive self-expression from the heart, ability to cheer up others in times of hardship and stress.

Habits—Feeling defined by how others react to them, needing praise to feel good.

☋ ♒ *North Node in Aquarius (rulers: Uranus, Saturn)*

Ideal—Detached and accurate vision.

Mistake—Cutting off from other people, which results in a lack of awareness of some important issues in situations, hence inaccuracy.

These are people who aim at freedom and are likely to cut themselves off from others in the process. The result can be a kind of lifelessness. Their assumption is that what they want must be what other people want, when they are in a group. It is their natural good humor and cheerfulness that create their friendships, and where they give their true warm affection, people are happy to accept their unusualness and sudden changes, and then they have the freedom they seek. Their heartfelt sincerity wins them listeners no matter how "off the wall" their ideas, and also gives them the courage to be different.

☋ ♍ *South Node in Virgo (ruler: Mercury)*

Skills—Ability to see where change would improve experience, ability to recognize what is most useful and what would be most helpful.

Habits—Criticizing automatically, too much self-criticism, perfectionism.

☊ ♓ *North Node in Pisces (rulers: Neptune, Jupiter)*

Ideal—Selfless service to humanity, strong intuitive/psychic ability.

Mistake—Fulfilling people's wishes rather than their needs, picking up everybody else's feelings and suffering from them.

These people long to merge with the things of the house that contains the Pisces North Node, but they lose themselves in the emotional or psychic process. They need to focus on what they are doing, being precise and discriminating in their work for others. As they learn to stop beating themselves and everyone else into an idea of perfection that is not in the moment, and do their best to be helpful to everyone they meet, they find that they are one with humanity as a whole. As they work at being unemotionally conscious of the unseen world, their psychic gifts unfold naturally.

☋ ♎ *South Node in Libra (ruler: Venus)*

Skills—Diplomacy, the ability to see the many sides of an issue, knowing when action is called for and which action is right.

Habits—Refusing to consider, or even recognize, an issue that requires action, being "nice" rather than honest.

☊ ♈ *North Node in Aries (ruler: Mars)*

Ideal—Knowing one's mind, fearless action in the right moment; recognizing one's self in the reflection.

Mistake—Acting impulsively, managing alone.

These people desire to do things their own way, thereby finding themselves. It can seem to them that this is impossible in a relationship. Rather than try to keep the peace, they need to use their diplomatic skills to express their truth and deal honestly with the consequent response. They will find the courage to be themselves only through their work in relationships, because they need the response and support of another to discover themselves.

☋ ♏ *South Node in Scorpio (rulers: Pluto, Mars)*

Skills—Deep sensitivity to their own and other people's emotions, determination and power to transform themselves.

Habits—Harboring emotional reactions without sharing them, leading to vengeful behavior.

☊ ♉ *North Node in Taurus (ruler: Venus)*

Ideal—To be steady, healthy, and secure.

Mistake—Trying to support others before steadying themselves.

These people are coming down to earth, and Nature will always be important to them. They aim to support others, being as steady as a rock, but other people's emotions trigger their instability and they can let people down. When they have plumbed the memories in their own emotional depths, they find their bedrock at the bottom. This is then their stable base, and no story, however desperate, will be able to shake that foundation.

☋ ♐ *South Node in Sagittarius (ruler: Jupiter)*

Skills—Ability to see the overview of any situation, natural philosophical understanding, ability to enthuse others.

Habits—Withholding from explaining their thoughts, having fun at another's expense.

☊ ♊ *North Node in Gemini (ruler: Mercury)*

Ideal—To be able to communicate with anyone.

Mistake—Talking about trivialities when no one is really interested.

These people can fall into the habit of chatting with people in a way that does not satisfy them. They need to be in touch with their natural philosophy so that their communications are interesting to them. The natural knowledge they are born with can be recognized by its obviousness when they first hear it. These people need to put their wisdom at people's service so that they communicate just that bit of the wider view that is relevant in the moment, and the satisfaction will be of discovering and encouraging everyone else's communication.

☋ ♑ South Node in Capricorn *(ruler: Saturn)*

Skills—Able to handle responsibility well, competent and effective.
Habits—Expecting others to work as hard as they do, allowing seriousness to become depression by not recognizing their feelings.

☊ ♋ North Node in Cancer *(ruler: the Moon)*

Ideal—To nurture the world through their caring.
Mistake—Holding on to those cared for, beyond usefulness.

These people need to take responsibility for their own experiences in life rather than become overburdened by responsibility for others. Once they realize that everyone needs to take responsibility for themselves, they can use their obvious abilities by teaching others with caring gentleness rather than doing things for them. They give the greatest gift by supporting people emotionally through the learning process, allowing them to make their own mistakes and go their own way. They find then that there is time to be playful, and can even share a child's lighthearted joy in life.

☋ ♒ South Node in Aquarius *(rulers: Uranus, Saturn)*

Skills—Ability to see clearly because of being detached.
Habits—Thinking that what is right for themselves must be right for everyone, not looking at their emotions.

☊ ♌ North Node in Leo *(ruler: the Sun)*

Ideal—To be one's self, to see the positive in every situation and person.
Mistake—Self-expression when not appropriate, resulting in experiences of rejection.

These people need to be in touch with who they are when on their own, so that they do not lose their center by trying to appeal to "the audience." Being alone without connecting to their truth will result in a hollow display when with others. Because this feels bad, they may cut off from others again, but if they will go through the pain of opening their heart and allowing others to see who they truly are, their genuine inner light will inspire all they meet.

☋ ♓ *South Node in Pisces (rulers: Neptune, Jupiter)*

Skills—Intuitive/psychic ability, empathizing with all others.
Habits—Not limiting their psychic space, which results in everyone being as affected by them as they are affected by others.

☊ ♍ *North Node in Virgo (ruler: Mercury)*

Ideal—Consciously working toward a better world for all.
Mistake—Thinking that there is one perfect way and that they know what it is.

These people need their natural awareness of how others feel so that their ways of helping are appropriate to each person and situation. In their efforts to improve a situation, they can easily criticize people, which can have the reverse effect. When they focus on the impressions they have of the whole situation, they will find that they intuitively know the best thing to say or do.

Ways in Which We Are Different

The North and South Nodes of the Moon, or intersection points that the Moon's path makes with the Sun's path, give us an axis across the chart drawn up for any moment in time. In a birth chart this axis can be interpreted as a direction that the person's spirit (Sun) gives to their personality (Moon) for this lifetime. There is, then, a sense of purpose or meaning to life when this direction is activated.

It is as though we unconsciously attract situations that call for the South Node activities by the house and style of the sign, while consciously trying to express the North Node activity and style. It isn't until we accept what is happening, and what skills we have, in the South Node area, that we find we are able to succeed in the North Node area. The way to reach the satisfaction promised by facing this direction is to use our South Node abilities to give to others, guided by our North Node ideals: to use our South Node skills to support our North Node aims.

Ruling Planets of the Nodes

Each Nodal Zodiac sign is ruled by a planet, as explained in chapter 3. The position of that ruling planet in the chart gives more information about how that Node is working for the person, whether they find it easy or have many difficulties associated with its activity, and whether it is in the forefront of their attention or working unconsciously in the background. The Nodal house is ruled by the planet ruling the sign on the house cusp, which may be the same as the Nodal sign. The house position of this planet, in addition to the Nodal house itself, gives us clues as to what activity will activate the Node.

When the ruler of the South Node is in the North Node sign, it indicates that the person may be part of the way toward making the desired development; it is as though the energy that was used in the old activities has been redirected to align with the new ideals, and there is less a tendency to pull back toward trying to be satisfied with the way things were.

The difficulty is gathering the courage to use that energy in situations that are new and that may seem daunting, especially as the planet will be weaker opposite its own rulership. For instance, let us look at people who have the South Node in Aries with Mars in the North Node sign in Libra; any habitual Aries aggression and thoughtlessness these people may feel will be tempered by a Libran consideration of others, which will be what they want to develop. But they may have difficulty getting their energy going and remembering that they can be independent. This difficulty will be emphasized if Mars conjuncts the North Node.

The ruler of the North Node in the South Node sign perhaps indicates that there is much to balance and recollect in the past, so that the alignment with the new direction will happen naturally when inner adjustments are made to situations that seem to recur. When the recurring reflection is recognized and accepted, these people will discover what attitude or assumption has been attracting it. Unhooking that thought from the unconscious releases energy, which can then be used to help others.

For instance, let us look at people who have Jupiter, as ruler of a Sagittarius North Node, in the South Node sign, Gemini. Here the expansive energy of Jupiter, which helps these people grow on the inside so that they can see more of the whole picture, tends to be occupied with all kinds of ideas that may distract them from their quest. Over and over they may find themselves too busy with disconnected activities to allow their ideas to develop. Perhaps they have been dependent on the praise they get for doing things for others, so when they register this thought and drop the compulsive behavior, they have the energy to communicate with real interest. The natural student/teacher arises in them; thus, the Sagittarian North Node is working.

Aspects to the Nodes

Aspects from planets to the Nodes indicate those parts of our personality that directly affect the unfolding of our path. They bring our growth or stagnation into daily importance. Often the Nodal path is unaspected. It will still function as described, but more as a background to life events. There will still be a sense of being stuck when we are off the path, and of satisfaction when we are on it, but not the emotional charge to either state.

Conjunction

A planet conjunct the South Node is an energy that we need to become aware of before our life will make sense. When the time comes in life to uncover the assumptions and regain the knowledge or skill, everything falls into place; our personal life will have meaning for us at last.

For instance, one way to interpret Uranus conjunct the South Node is that there may have been some loss or separation in the past that may have been more painful than we want to accept. Unless we accept it, the Uranian energy can be seen as cutting the entire experience out of our memory. If we refuse part of an old lifetime, or repress early experiences in this life, we are unable to claim the skills we learned there. So if we reject this painful memory, we cannot use the skill that was part of our qualities during the painful sequence. Because the South Node also shows the tools we need, that skill would be most helpful to us in dealing with our life. When we retrieve the memory, we can then use the skill, and meaning comes back to our life.

A planet conjunct the North Node represents an energy that comes into play as soon as we align with our Nodal direction. We tend to feel this energy as a quality that does not belong to us. After the first effort to claim it, we become apprehensive about using that energy, because it seems that we are unable to maintain it. Other people seem to find that kind of behavior easy, and we doubt ourselves because it seems so difficult for us in comparison. We look for people who can do it, projecting the energy onto them, and feeling ourselves incapable of being the way they are; yet when we risk it, we find it is favorably received.

We will, of course, feel incomplete until we follow our Nodal direction and integrate the planetary energy connected with it, and the best way to do this is by deliberately sorting out the habits and collecting the abilities of the South Node. The ruler of the sign containing the North Node and planet will show a way in which we may overcome our apprehension through becoming involved with activities relevant to its position.

For instance, let's look at Venus conjunct the North Node in Pisces. These people may lack a sense of being able to relate well. Other people seem able to relate so much better, whereas they get lost trying to be what others want. These people have to go back to the Virgo South Node and rediscover their conscious focus, their ability to discriminate, in order to reclaim a self-contained point of view. Then they will be able to see what people really need, and the house containing Neptune, ruler of Pisces, will show in what activity they are best equipped to use their intuition to serve people well. This kind of relating will satisfy them more than simply trying to please.

Square

A planet square to both Nodes operates like a distraction from the Nodal path. We get into that energy and then feel stuck. It can feel like a conflict of interests, where we can see ourselves getting in our own way. One way to look at it is that we need an extra ability on the path that is not directly linked with it, so we have to go "off course" to learn it. When that work is done, we return to the path enriched.

There is a tendency to go off the path into the activity of the squaring planet whenever things get difficult, until the inner urge for growth drives us back again. Also there can be a sense that life "disapproves of" the expression of that planetary energy, the style and preferred activities of that part of our nature.

It can be helpful to contemplate how the side of us represented by the squaring planet actually assists our Nodal direction; we may discover that a squaring Mars represents the courage to delve into the past, and to face the unknown future, as long as we do not fall into negative use of the energy. A squaring Saturn, while feeling like circumstances are preventing our direction, can stop us from starting things too soon; if we hold to our course and accept that it will take time and that there will be lessons to learn on the way, the Saturn will reflect our sense of steady determination with which we can achieve almost anything.

Trine

A planet that trines one Node necessarily sextiles the other. When a planet trines the South Node, it indicates a natural ability to use that planetary characteristic. For instance, Jupiter trine the South Node will indicate a natural generosity and openness that is part of our old skills. Sextile the North Node, this Jupiter quality will help us unfold our direction by attracting opportunities for growth that we can choose.

A planet trining the North Node represents an energy that helps us unfold our potential, encouraging us to keep going forward. It is a characteristic that gives us confidence to approach our future, and its house indicates activities that will take us forward without us consciously trying. We may need to focus this energy consciously on the South Node area, in order to sort out what we are still bringing with us from the past. Otherwise, we may rush into our direction, trailing and tripping over habits that are no longer appropriate. For instance, Mercury trine the North Node indicates people who know what their direction is and focus their conscious thinking on that. Searching out any unconscious expectations will help prevent them from recreating the past.

A Personal Path Through Life

Our direction in life gives a purpose for all our experiences, and a meaning for all our efforts. There are many ways of interpreting the Nodes in a birth chart, and it is extremely important that the direction as described should feel right to the person receiving it. It may be best to hint at what it might be and allow each person's own sense of joy and satisfaction to discover what it might truly be.

Our path through life is not only absolutely individual to each of us, it is also subject to change, to unfolding, and even to complete transformation. It is a direction, not a goal that can be achieved, but there will be many satisfying achievements on the way. Once our feet are on that personal path, the spirit that we truly are is a constant companion, and all of life is lit with an inner confidence.

The Nodal axis is a direction that we face. In standing, as it were, on the rim of our experience, looking across the wheel of life to the other side, we are also facing the hub at the center. Our effort to activate the North Node, while accepting all that we are in the South Node, draws us into the center. In other words, we need only accept all that we are in the moment in order to relax into the light that is in our center, and radiate the spirit that we really are.

Conclusion

In essence, each person is one whole being, not divisible into parts. One whole cannot be divided into parts any more than that which is alive can be divided from the Source of life. In complementary therapies, the "whole person" is considered for treatment. In astrology, we also look at the whole person; but to do this, all systems appear to divide that person into spirit, mind, attitudes, emotions, body, direction, surroundings, and so on.

In order to speak about our experiences and our differences from each other, we divide ourselves into many levels. For example, we look at emotions independently from the body even though they are two expressions of the same thing, the hormones being an obvious link, but also muscle tension, body posture, and so on.

Similarly, we divide spirit from the mind, automatic reactions from considered responses, male from female behaviors, inner child from responsible adult, until we feel like a chaotic assortment of bits and pieces that are impossible to integrate.

The essence that we are, which is expressed at so many different levels, cannot be wholly described from any one of these parts, and it is important to remember that all we are doing is describing the whole from many different perspectives, each view of limited value, and of no value at all unless seen as an aspect of the whole itself. The beauty of astrology is that its language is comprised of symbols and patterns, which can be read at any of the levels, giving us a sense of the unchanging essence.

It is the personality that has trouble, not the spirit: trouble with negative expression of opposite signs, difficult aspects between planets, and anxiety about the North Node direction. The personality finds some Zodiac signs difficult to understand, and cannot see how it could possibly get on with others. But the spirit understands perfectly and dances with everything in the chart, with all the Zodiac signs at once.

The Center of the Circle

Each of us contains the qualities of all twelve signs, the energy of every planet, and the windows on life of all twelve houses. Bearing this in mind, all twelve Nodal directions combine in every one of us.

As we look from the South Nodes toward the corresponding North Nodes, we are, in fact, facing across the center, and it becomes a movement from outside to within: from the experiences we have of life, astrologically pictured around a circle as planets in signs in houses, to the point in the center of the "circle and cross" of our chart.

That center point is the point of transformation where we fall through into the truth of our eternal unified Being—Oneness.

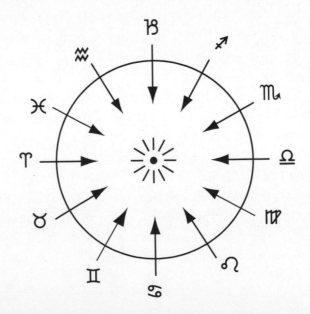

Index

For readers of

Soul Purpose Astrology

only

FREE Natal Chart Offer

Thank you for purchasing *Soul Purpose Astrology*. There are a number of ways to construct a chart wheel. The easiest way, of course, is by computer, and that's why we are giving you this one-time offer of a free natal chart. This extremely accurate chart will provide you with a great deal of information about yourself. Once you receive a chart from us, *Soul Purpose Astrology* will show you how to view character traits and learning experiences in a positive and transformative way, and gain a better understanding of your life's highest purpose.

Also, by ordering your free chart, you will be enrolled in Llewellyn's Birthday Club! From now on, you can get any of Llewellyn's astrology reports for 25% off when you order within one month of your birthday! Just write "Birthday Club" on your order form or mention it when ordering by phone. As if that wasn't enough, we will mail you a FREE copy of our fresh new book *What Astrology Can Do for You!* Go for it!

Complete this form with your accurate birth data and mail it to us today. Enjoy your adventure in self-discovery through astrology!

Do not photocopy this form. Only this original will be accepted.

Please Print

Full Name:_____

Mailing
Address:_____

City, State,
Zip:_____

Birth time:_____ A.M. P.M. (please circle)

Month:_____ Day:_____ Year:_____

Birthplace (city, county, state, country):

_____

_____

Check your birth certificate for the most accurate information.
Complete and mail this form to: Llewellyn Publications, Special Chart Offer, P.O. Box 64383, 0-7387-0221-8, St. Paul, MN 55164.
Allow 4–6 weeks for delivery.

*Llewellyn publishes hundreds of books
on your favorite subjects.*

LOOK FOR THE CRESCENT MOON
to find the one you've been searching for!

MULTICULTURAL
MAGICK

To find the book you've been searching for, just call or write for a FREE copy of our full-color catalog, *New Worlds of Mind & Spirit*. *New Worlds* is brimming with books and other resources to help you develop your magical and spiritual potential to the fullest! Explore over 80 exciting pages that include:

- Exclusive interviews, articles and "how-tos" by Llewellyn's expert authors

- Features on classic Llewellyn books

- Tasty previews of Llewellyn's latest books on astrology, Tarot, Wicca, shamanism, magick, the paranormal, spirituality, mythology, alternative health and healing, and more

- Monthly horoscopes by Gloria Star

- Plus special offers available only to *New Worlds* readers

To get your free *New Worlds* catalog, call
1-877-NEW-WRLD

or send your name and address to

Llewellyn
P.O. Box 64383
St. Paul, MN 55164-0383

Visit our web site at www.llewellyn.com

LLEWELLYN
New Worlds of Mind and Spirit